# When Did We See You?

*A Lenten Exploration of Poverty & Wealth*

Elizabeth Mae Magill

Nashville

WHEN DID WE SEE YOU? A Lenten Exploration of Poverty & Wealth



ISBN: 978-0-8358-2084-4

Epub ISBN: 978-0-8358-2085-1

Cover design: Faceout Studio

Interior design: PerfecType, Nashville, TN

For more information on resources available from The Upper Room

call 1-800-972-0433 or visit www.upperroom.org

*To the Poor People's Campaign*

# Table of Contents

Chapter 1: Lent . . . . . . . . . . . . . . . . . . . . . . . . . . . . . . . . . . . 5

Chapter 2: Material Poverty . . . . . . . . . . . . . . . . . . . . . . . . 17

Chapter 3: Wealth . . . . . . . . . . . . . . . . . . . . . . . . . . . . . . . . 39

Chapter 4: Spiritual Poverty . . . . . . . . . . . . . . . . . . . . . . . . 63

Chapter 5: Charity . . . . . . . . . . . . . . . . . . . . . . . . . . . . . . . 83

Chapter 6: Justice . . . . . . . . . . . . . . . . . . . . . . . . . . . . . . 105

Chapter 7: Connections . . . . . . . . . . . . . . . . . . . . . . . . . . .133

Epilogue: Easter Morning . . . . . . . . . . . . . . . . . . . . . . . . .155

Acknowledgments. . . . . . . . . . . . . . . . . . . . . . . . . . . . . . .157

# Lent

## My Story

"Where will you go on your honeymoon?" Ricardo asked. He's one of the regulars at our street church. Sometimes he has housing and sometimes he stays at the shelter downtown.

"France."

"Wow!" His eyes got very big. "We went to West Brookfield to the antique shops," he offered, mentioning a town forty minutes west of here.

"My cousin lives in Paris. We will stay with him," I quickly added. I was almost apologizing for the apparent extravagance.

"Wow!" he replied again.

On a gorgeous, hot Sunday afternoon in August, Ken and I got married on Worcester Common. I wore a purple dress I'd made and held flowers my best friend had gathered. We said "I do" in a ceremony embedded into our regular outdoor worship service. Afterward, we hung out visiting and enjoying the weekly lunch brought by a nearby indoor church. A few people brought wedding gifts—a plush toy, a pencil holder made from an orange juice can, a box of chocolates—and everyone offered their best hopes for our future. Worcester Fellowship is a church composed of parishioners without homes as well as those at risk of homelessness. I was the pastor there at that time, and the congregation was thrilled I was getting married with them on the common—a simple wedding woven into the regular weekly pattern.

This lovely example of simplicity hid the fact that we'd had a huge wedding the day before, complete with a rented tent, live music, and a catered buffet for two hundred guests with three different entrees. And while we weren't hiding the fact that we were honeymooning in France, we weren't exactly advertising it.

Every week, our parishioners would share the stories of their lives and their struggles, but as a leader in the congregation, I found it hard to speak about my own life. It was even awkward to take time off—paid time off—when our parishioners did not get benefits like that from their work.

What should I have said about my extravagant travel plans? I mean, we weren't over the top (I say defensively to you, reader). We stayed with my cousin who lived in Paris. We used frequent flyer miles. We went to an inexpensive bed and breakfast in the countryside. We took the train. On top of that, our friends and family generously donated to our trip, which we took a year later to spread out the expenses.

None of these "cost saving" decisions would have been possible for the people we were worshiping with on that Sunday afternoon. Paid vacation time? Miles accumulated by flying *elsewhere*? Savings for emergencies, a growing retirement plan, and enough left over to spend *three weeks* in France? Yeah, right.

I founded Worcester Fellowship in 2007 along with a seminary friend to provide worship, lunch, and pastoral care to adults without homes and those at risk of homelessness. We had integrated weddings into the worship service before, so when my husband and I decided to marry I knew I'd include a worship service with these beloved parishioners.

But it was awkward to be someone with more than enough while serving this congregation. For years I'd argued to my co-pastor that if we are too embarrassed to say what we are doing for vacation, we shouldn't do it. But now it was my turn to take a big trip, and I was both embarrassed . . . and still going. What does it mean to have that kind of wealth? What does it mean to be a Christian with money? What *should* I be doing with the money that I have?

I expect that the conversations spurred by the pages that follow will be deeply uncomfortable. To be honest, it has been a deeply uncomfortable topic to write about. As a result of writing this book, my husband and I have talked about some hard truths regarding money and made several changes to our own finances.

We have never been spendthrifts. While we pay attention to our financial decisions, we haven't exactly chosen to maximize our income (I am a pastor after all). But the fact that we don't obsess over or worship money doesn't mean we don't have a lot of it—and it doesn't mean that we're okay with letting it go. Like ordinary middle-class Americans, we worry about having enough for retirement, enough if the economy goes astray, and enough if one or both of us gets seriously ill.

This book chronicles my own internal struggle with what our Christian faith says about money and poverty—what to do with our wealth, and what to do about poverty in our church, our town, and our nation. This Lent, I want to consider how my wealth might keep me from God, and I invite you to join me.

## Why Lent?

Several traditions and concepts gave rise to what we now call Lent. Sometime between the third and fourth centuries, the traditions of pre-Easter fasting and the ritualistic preparation time for Christians who were about to be baptized merged into one forty-day practice based around Jesus' own forty-day experience in the wilderness following his baptism.[1] The practices of Lent have continued to evolve in the millennium and a half since. For example, community fasting and introspection have become a private decision to "give something up for Lent." The educational component morphed from daily afternoon sermons to weekly Lenten studies.[2]

But some things have also stayed the same. Early catechumens were asked to decide if they wanted to take on the obligations of Christian living. This study asks similar questions: What are the Christian obligations to those who are poor? Do we want to take on those obligations? How do our material possessions influence our closeness—or distance from—God?

In 1966, Pope Paul VI reaffirmed that Lent's purpose is penance, practiced through prayer, fasting, and charity. However, he also offered an important shift. The pope emphasized that witnessing through asceticism and denial is essential in places where economic prosperity prevails. In contrast, he suggested that God would accept the existing suffering of those living in poverty as their sacrificial gift.[3] While everyone is called to prayer and works of charity and social justice, only the wealthy and comfortable should deny themselves materially.

This contrast between self-denial as an act of penance and denial as a fact of life raises challenging questions. This Lent, I want to focus on these questions about wealth and poverty and what these reveal about faith. I want to talk to others at my church and in my

---

1. Andrew B. McGowan, *Ancient Christian Worship: Early Church Practices in Social, Historical, and Theological Perspective* (Grand Rapids, MI: Baker Academic, 2014), 240-242.

2. McGowan, *Ancient Christian Worship*, 98.

3. Paul VI, *Apostolic Constitution Paenitemini of the Supreme Pontiff Paul VI on Fast and Abstinence* (Dicastero per la Comunicazione—Libreria Editrice Vaticana, 1966), Chapter III. https://www.vatican.va/content/paul-vi/en/apost_constitutions/documents/hf_p-vi_apc_19660217_paenitemini.html. Accessed March 28, 2025.

family about the struggle to live authentically as Christians in the face of inequality. As Easter approaches, we face challenging questions: Will we choose to renew our baptismal vows? Does doing so require giving up all or some of our material comforts? What one or two changes can we make regarding wealth and poverty that will bring us closer to God?

## Ash Wednesday

Lent begins with Ash Wednesday, a day when we are reminded we are made of dust and will return to dust. The day focuses on our physical existence—we are bodies, created by God from the dust of the earth. From this awareness of our physical nature, it's only a small step to begin considering our material needs.

On this day, those who are poor can rest in God's blessing and assurance that we all deserve basic material resources: food, housing, and healthcare. For those who have more than they need, today presents an opportunity to ask how to share their material wealth. All of us can draw closer to God by recognizing that God has given us physical bodies with material needs and that all of our bodies deserve care.

The scriptures the lectionary assigns to Ash Wednesday turn us to the prophets: Isaiah 58:1-12 and Joel 2:1-2, 12-17. The Isaiah passage calls on both the prophet and us to lift our voices in warning to those who seek God yet have broken the covenant relationship. The text calls out those who fast and appear to humble themselves while, at the same time, oppressing workers and stirring up conflict.

God's not having any of that. Don't put ashes on your head and wear mournful clothing if you aren't going to live up to the covenant. What God wants instead is this: an end to injustice, an end to oppression, and the elimination of the heavy burdens of poverty—homelessness, hunger, and inadequate healthcare.

In Joel, the land has been destroyed by an army (whether of locusts or human soldiers remains unclear). The people are in despair. God calls them to turn back toward God—not by tearing their clothes as a grand gesture but by tearing their hearts. They are instructed to fast in the hope that God will rescue them from devastation.

When people lack material resources—in this case, crops to eat—our hearts should break.

Yet Isaiah calls for more than broken hearts; he demands action to restore the streets of the city and the land that provides for it.

> Your ancient ruins shall be rebuilt;
> you shall raise up the foundations of many generations;
> you shall be called the repairer of the breach,
> the restorer of streets to live in.—Isaiah 58:12

With these words, Lent begins with a call to repair the neighborhoods in which we live.

One example of putting these words into action comes from the organization Repairers of the Breach. The Rev. Dr. William Barber founded Repairers of the Breach in 2015 to make room for and amplify the voices of the oppressed to bring about change. This began in North Carolina, then spread throughout the United States. Their mostly widely known actions were "Moral Mondays," state house protests asking state governments to respond to the needs of the poor.

This concept of repairing the breach and restoring the places where we live has become one of the foundations of the Poor People's Campaign. This national campaign works with state coordinating committees to elect national leaders who will prioritize the needs of the poor. The goal is to focus not on left and right, but on the moral call to care for our community.

Like the words of Isaiah and Joel, the Poor People's Campaign is overtly political. Its message addresses our nation and our government, calling them to care for the poor. As Lent begins, the ashes on our foreheads remind us of our calling and obligation to do this work and care for the bodies of God's people.

## Conclusion

Ash Wednesday marks the beginning of a time of reflection. This year, we are reflecting on how our material lives—whether wealth or poverty—influence our interior lives. We are looking for what we must confess, what we must change, and how we might live more faithful lives. In the coming chapters, we will take the time to think about our material resources and our faith. We will think about how we care for others and how we remain dependent on God. It will be an interesting journey.

## LENTEN REFLECTIONS

### A DAILY PRAYER FOR THE FIRST WEEK OF LENT

Holy one, help us to see you more closely during this Lenten season. Help us to see ourselves, to recognize our place in this world you have given us. Forgive us for the ways we close our eyes to material poverty. Holy one, help us to see you in all whom we meet. Amen.

### FIRST WEEK OF LENT

#### WEDNESDAY REFLECTIONS • Ashes

What does the idea of ashes symbolize for you? How do you connect to your body, and how does having a body connect you to God? Do you love the physicalness of the body God created for you? What do you think about on a holy day meant to remind us of death? When you think about death, an afterlife, and your relationship to God, what comes to mind? Who do you remember when you think about death?

#### THURSDAY REFLECTIONS • Fasting

What have you given up or added on during Lent in years past? What meaning did you make from this form of fasting? Have you tried intentionally adding or removing material things at other times? Did this help you connect to God? If so, how did this help you connect to God? If not, what issues arose?

#### FRIDAY REFLECTIONS • Penitence

What does it feel like to spend time being penitent? Do you bear guilt easily, or is it something you can release? Do you feel forgiven when a person offers forgiveness? What about when God offers forgiveness? For you, is penitence more about a thought, a feeling, or an action? What are some practices that might help you feel satisfaction with penitence?

## SATURDAY REFLECTIONS • Charity

What do you think of when you consider charity? Are you generally a charitable person? Is there a way that Christian charity is a distinctive form of charity? We often consider it an obligation to give charity. Is there a similar obligation to receive it? What are some non-material forms of charity?

## SUNDAY REFLECTIONS • Faith

How does the Lenten season affect your faith? How does it affect your prayer life? What for you is the value of forty days of reflection time? Do you find Lenten interior reflections lead to outward changes in your life? Is there something you wish were part of Lent? Do you engage with different music, art, or study during Lent?

## ASH WEDNESDAY LITANY

Ash Wednesday worship typically includes a litany of confession or repentance before the distribution of ashes. The following prayer can be used to supplement or replace traditional litanies with one that focuses on material poverty.

### PRAYER OF CONFESSION

Forgive us, God, for the ways we have failed to serve the poor and failed to end poverty. Forgive us for the inequality of our community.

**We confess our sins and ask for forgiveness.**

Forgive us, God, for the times we look away and for the relationships we have failed to initiate. Forgive us for failing to stand in solidarity with those who do not have enough.

**We confess our sins and ask for forgiveness.**

Forgive us, God, for the times we assume that poverty is inevitable. Forgive us for the ways we ignore inequality and sit comfortably with the status quo.

**We confess our sins and ask for forgiveness.**

Forgive us, God, for the times we hold too tightly to what we have, letting possessions keep us from others and from you. Forgive us for our endless accumulation.

**We confess our sins and ask for forgiveness.**

*Allow for a time of silent confession.*

Restore us, God, and redeem us in your eyes. Guide us to be your people, attentive to the poor among us. Guide us to care for all those in need and to release what we do not need.

# INTERLUDE

## Worcester Fellowship

Worcester Fellowship is only one of more than one hundred street churches in the Ecclesia Ministry network. Each is specific to its context, but the basics are worship, food, and pastoral care for people who are homeless or at risk of homelessness. We are primarily focused on *church* and connecting people to God and to one another, but we also, of course, help connect our parishioners to services available in the community.

Typically, twenty to thirty people worship as part of Worcester Fellowship, which is followed by a lunch for around sixty in the winter and over one hundred in the summer. Churches with buildings sign up in advance to provide lunch for the community.

At Worcester Fellowship, our lunch line is just like church. Sometimes, it feels rigid and full of rules. I hate the kind of "Let's keep you in your place" mentality that these feelings breed. But other times, it reflects the positive side of church, filled with hopefulness and community. I love the bonds built in that line and the underlying promise of abundance provided by the lunch offerings.

At the start of our ministry, I loved the symbolism of the altar as the way to shape our lunches. I thought about a pile of sandwiches as a placeholder for the bread and juice of Communion. It was a great visual, but over the years, the community voted to shift toward a more straightforward routine, and they really wanted a line—a strict, no cutting, first-come, first-served lunch line. This didn't alleviate the chaos of a big group meal. People still arrive late, ask friends to hold their place, and leave to smoke then try to rejoin where they were. There are always plenty of sandwiches and snack bags, but your place in the line still matters. People at the front of the line might get tuna salad, while people at the end might get bologna or peanut butter and jelly.

"I'm hoping for tuna" says Sam, who is always a little late and a little anxious. He's also always in need of lunch for both himself and his girlfriend. "Will there be any tuna when I get to the front of the line?" he asks.

I don't know the answer. I never know the answer. But before I can tell him (again) that I don't know what the visiting church has brought, I recognize the beginning of a fight ahead of us in the line. An older Latino man I don't know says quietly but firmly, "Hey, don't cut," and I head toward the problem.

My stole identifies my place of authority. It flaps in the wind as I support the man in the line keeping the rules I hate to enforce. I look at the other man and tell him he has to go to the back of the line. In response, this very angry young white man tightens his fists at his side and says, "I haven't eaten in days."

I nod sympathetically and point to the end of the line, but he stomps around and plops down dramatically on one of the park benches muttering, "Well then I won't eat."

Harvey, a regular at both lunch and worship, and a good line-abiding Christian who cannot contain his anger at this blatant disregard for the rules: "Why do you always cut the line? Why can't you go to the end of the line?" This does not help. The young man jumps back up screaming, "I'll go anywhere I damn well please," before adding "Why don't you mind your own business?"

As we talk, the line snakes forward, all of us getting closer to the sandwiches. When Robert, waiting five or six people ahead of all this arguing, reaches the food table, he takes a sandwich, an orange, a bag of chips, and a box of juice and hands them to the screaming young man. Robert, the humble repairer in the breach, then quietly moves back to the end of the line to get his own lunch, probably peanut butter and jelly this time.

# Material Poverty

## My Story

I started life poor. My dad worked at the shipyard in Norfolk, Virginia, then tried going back to school, then tried selling pots and pans door to door. He was required to buy the demonstration set as a sales tool. We still have the entire set, minus one pan bought by a woman who felt sorry for him. My mom worked as a social worker—a job she lost once she was visibly pregnant.

I was born with two hernias. My mom remembers that when I laughed, the subsequent pain would make me cry. When my parents met with the surgeon who explained the procedure I needed, my dad told him, "We don't have any way to pay for this." They were completely broke.

"I'll take your payment when you get on your feet again," the surgeon replied.

The doctor who delivered me heard their story and offered similar grace saying, "Have your kids when you are young and poor. Pay me when you are older."

But not everyone was so understanding. When my dad explained his situation to a credit card collections agency, he got no sympathy. He had a (tiny!) unpaid balance of $2.46. Sixty years later, Dad is still angry, "They told me to make a partial payment!" We survived those times by scrimping, going without, and eating with other relatives or at church dinners.

When I was five, my dad finally landed a good job that took us to a new state. We bought a home and settled into a working-class neighborhood. Dad worked nights, while Mom cared for my sister, brother, and neighborhood children in our home. When people envision an idyllic portrait of working-class life, they're probably imagining my life in that neighborhood. We played outside with other kids; we went on camping vacations, and were careful with our money. We made decisions based on what we could afford and when we could afford it. We struggled, but my memory is of a loving, happy family.

Working-class language and values are embedded within me. Yet my story always included a sense of hope—a feeling that we would soon have more, that an improved future awaited us, that getting ahead was always possible if we would keep-on-keeping-on. For my family, that hopeful future turned out to be true.

From that time on, my childhood was marked by steadily increasing stability and, eventually, modest wealth. Though I experienced poverty again—after college and once more following a divorce combined with job loss—the safety nets of savings, education, family support, and accumulated confidence meant I was never as poor as I had been at birth.

## Liberation Theology

I didn't really think about poverty or working-class identities, I just lived my life. But as I got older, the churches I attended, and then seminary, introduced me to the concept of liberation theology. Liberation theology holds that God's message is primarily one of freedom for those who are poor and oppressed. In Luke 4:16-21, Jesus begins his ministry by repeating the words of the prophet Isaiah:

"The Spirit of the Lord is upon me,
because he has anointed me
to bring good news to the poor.
He has sent me to proclaim release to the captives
and recovery of sight to the blind,
to set free those who are oppressed
to proclaim the year of the Lord's favor."—Luke 4:18-19

Jesus' ministry is good news for those who are poor and oppressed. Gustavo Gutiérrez described this as God's preferential option for the poor in his book *A Theology of Liberation: History, Politics, and Salvation.* Poverty, Gutiérrez argues, dehumanizes us, distorting God's creation. This is incompatible with God's rule. God wants all people to live with dignity.[4] The promise of release found in Luke (and Isaiah) becomes our mandate today—as the body of Christ, we are called to carry out the work of liberation in our communities.

## Mark 14:3-9: The Poor Will Always Be with You

When you imagine a study on poverty, what are the first scriptures that come to mind? For me, I immediately think of Jesus saying, "The poor are always with you." What exactly does that mean? What is Jesus saying here? The statement certainly seems true, but its meaning runs deeper.

The story where Jesus says this begins with a woman, possibly a wealthy woman or at least a woman who was in possession of a jar of very expensive perfume. While Jesus is sitting at the dinner table, the woman pours the contents of the jar on Jesus. When some of the other guests complain about the waste, Jesus responds that they will always have the poor with them:

---

4. Gustavo Gutiérrez, *A Theology of Liberation: History, Politics, and Salvation* (15th anniversary edition, Orbis, 1988), translated by Sister Caridad Inda and John Eagleson, 167, 168.

> While he was at Bethany in the house of Simon the leper, as he sat at the table, a woman came with an alabaster jar of very costly ointment of nard, and she broke open the jar and poured the ointment on his head. But some were there who said to one another in anger, Why was the ointment wasted in this way? For this ointment could have been sold for more than three hundred denarii and the money given to the poor. And they scolded her. But Jesus said, "Let her alone; why do you trouble her? She has performed a good service for me. For you always have the poor with you, and you can show kindness to them whenever you wish, but you will not always have me. She has done what she could; she has anointed my body beforehand for its burial. Truly I tell you, wherever the good news is proclaimed in the whole world, what she has done will be told in remembrance of her."—Mark 14:3-9

This story continues a theme throughout the Gospels: Jesus as a boundary-breaker. His choices—staying with a leper, eating with tax collectors, and allowing this woman to anoint him—all violated the rules of his time. Even viewing himself worthy of this indulgent gift is boundary breaking.

The timing is also significant. This event happens just before Jesus' trials in Jerusalem, and the anointing carries a dual meaning. It could signify either the coronation of a king or the preparation of a body for burial. The point of the story is not actually about the poor but about recognizing Jesus' importance. Perhaps the message is we can be lavish in caring for those who are suffering. Perhaps the story grants us permission for the extravagant celebration of someone we love.

The more cynical side of me suggests that Jesus intends to expose the hypocrisy of those complaining. They didn't use their money to care for the poor yesterday, and they probably won't tomorrow either. The woman's decision to anoint him doesn't stop anyone from fulfilling their obligations to the poor. Jesus' statement echoes Deuteronomy 15:11: "Since there will never cease to be some in need on earth, I therefore command you, 'Open your hand to the poor and needy neighbor in your land.'" Deuteronomy explicitly commands that resources *should* go to the poor; it names the ongoing need precisely to encourage us to care. Jesus adds that we *always* have this opportunity.[5] This is a pointed jab and an observation that we often ignore. It makes the complaints of the guests—and, on occasion, our own complaints—ring hollow.

Certainly, Jesus is not saying it is *good* that the poor will always be with us. The existence of the poor is not an excuse for our bad behavior. We can always choose, as God commands throughout the Bible, to care for those who are poor.

## Who Are the Poor?

To respond faithfully to God's call, we must first understand who "the poor" are in our context. In the United States, there are two primary ways we talk about household poverty. The first approach compares a household's income against an income threshold commonly referred to as the "poverty line," which is defined as the minimum amount of income deemed necessary to maintain a basic standard of living. In 2025, the poverty line for a four-person household is $32,150. For one person, the line is $15,650.[6] Government benefit programs are often directly tied to the poverty line. However, these programs recognize that the official threshold often underestimates

---

5. Pheme Perkins, "The Gospel of Mark," in Leander Keck et al., *The New Interpreters Bible* Volume VII (Nashville: Abingdon Press, 1995), 698.
6. Office of the Assistant Secretary for Planning and Evaluation, ASPE, "Poverty Guidelines," https://aspe.hhs.gov/topics/poverty-economic-mobility/poverty-guidelines. Accessed March 3, 2025.

real need and tend to be available for those who make up to 150 percent of the poverty line (and occasionally as high as 200 percent).

In 2023, just over twelve percent of people lived in households below the poverty line. According to the raw numbers, most poor Americans are white (by a large margin), women (by a small margin), employed, high-school educated, and between 35 and 64 years old.

However, these raw numbers mask other significant disparities. While a large majority of those below the poverty line are white, only one in ten white households live in poverty. In stark contrast, one in five Black and Native American households are impoverished. Similarly, one in six Hispanic/Latino households exist below the poverty line. Education creates another major divide—one in four people without a high school diploma live in poverty, while this is true only for one out of every twenty-five people with a college degree.[7]

The second means for evaluating poverty divides U.S. households into income quintiles—five equal segments each with twenty percent of the population. Household income includes all sources of income: Social Security, government programs, pensions, investment income, and, of course, income from employment. Also of note is that this quintile system does not account for household size.

In 2022, the lowest one-fifth of the U.S. population took in less than $30,000, with an average income of $16,120. The second lowest group earned between $30,000 and $58,020 with an average of $43,850.[8] While most households in the second quintile have incomes above the official poverty line, many in this group still struggle financially.

Of course, poverty is also contextual, both geography and household size determine whether these incomes provide stability.

---

7. United States Census Bureau, https://data.census.gov/table/ACSST1Y2023.S1701. Accessed March 29, 2025.

8. Tax Policy Center Urban Institute & Brookings Institution, https://taxpolicycenter.org/statistics/household-income_quintiles. Accessed March 28, 2025.

A family of four living in Boston would face serious struggles on $43,850 a year, while a single person in rural Iowa might live comfortably on that amount.

Given these variations, income alone may not be the best measure of material poverty. Instead, stability might be a better indicator: Do you have access to the housing, food, water, and healthcare that you need? Or more precisely, do you have access to *decent* housing and *healthy* food? For some, the dividing line between poverty and the middle class is homeownership, though mortgage costs can also be the very thing that pushes someone's expenses beyond their available income.

Growing up, I was taught that housing should consume no more than twenty-five percent of my income, though today thirty percent is considered reasonable. To break it down for you, a yearly income of $43,850 translates to $3,654 per month. To meet that thirty percent limit, rent plus utilities would need to stay below $1,100 monthly. As discussed earlier, that might be possible in some places, especially for a single person, but it's borderline impossible for others, especially families living in large cities. I once knew a woman whose mental health issues made it difficult for her to find a room to rent. In addition, she had a felony record that barred her from subsidized housing. She was thrilled to find an apartment that consumed 90% of her income! While I'm glad she found somewhere to live, that is not stable or sustainable. She is not alone in this struggle.

While researchers often identify income and housing costs as the primary determinants of poverty, many other factors affect a person's stability. For instance, childcare is notoriously expensive and can cause serious issues for working parents. Additionally, some people have parents or other extended family that live with them and depend on their income. Households that include people with significant disabilities may find themselves poor even with incomes in the third or fourth quintile. Medical emergencies, long-term healthcare, and home nursing services can all rapidly deplete savings, pushing elderly households from stability to poverty almost overnight. While a person's regular income might cover the basics of life, those basics are rarely the only responsibilities someone carries.

## Generational Poverty

Regardless of family size, a serious illness costing $10,000 or even $20,000 out of pocket will devastate any household making $43,850 annually. It could easily devastate a household making far more. This vulnerability reveals perhaps the most important distinction between the middle class and the poor: resilience in the face of crisis. Can you save money for emergencies? Is your employment stable and predictable? Does your job provide healthcare and retirement benefits, or do you need to purchase them separately and at an additional expense? Can you absorb sudden expenses needed for the care of your child or parent?

These questions about handling emergencies lead directly to the issue of generational poverty. When a crisis strikes, do you have family or friends you can turn to who can provide material support? When I earned just $13,000 a year as a part-time chemistry teacher, my parents had stable jobs and a nearly paid-off mortgage. This enabled them to help my siblings and me launch our adult lives. My sister even provided the downpayment for my first house.

Poverty often means lacking this crucial support system. Sometimes, support evaporates because addictions or mental health struggles strain relationships, but more often, families simply do not have extra funds to share. A few hundred dollars can mean the difference between stability and crisis—a car repair that saves a job, a deposit that secures housing. Without access to these "small" payments, people spiral deeper and deeper into debt while their medical or emotional crises worsen.

Nothing benefits a low-income household more than family members who are both willing and able to share. A stable childhood, the promise of a college education, music lessons, gymnastics classes, summer camp—none of these guarantee a life without poverty, but they all help to one degree or another.

## A Story

I was sitting at *common art*, the weekly gathering that's part of *common cathedral*, a street church in Boston. Every week, we meet at a local church to make art together. Acrylic paints and canvases were strewn across a large round table protected by thin plastic sheeting. Sue and Ana wore oversized men's shirts as makeshift aprons and chatted while they painted. Like most of those present, they had stowed their backpacks—containing all their belongings—in a corner of the room.

"Where is Caleb?" Sue asked.

"I haven't seen him in a while," Ana responded before pausing to rinse her brush. "Did you hear he won the lottery?"

"Get out!"

"Like $10,000!" Ana scooped up a glob of red paint with her brush and returned to her canvas. "My whole life would be different with $10,000."

The conversation then drifted from speculation about Caleb's whereabouts to dreams of what they would do if they won the lottery. Meanwhile, my internal dialogue turned judgmental: *They have no idea how little difference $10,000 would make. Spend your money on the lottery, and you'll never get ahead. Ten thousand dollars would be nice, but how would it change someone's life?*

I was new to street ministry and knew little about money—especially how transformative a $10,000 windfall could be for someone living in poverty. But I was beginning to learn.

## The Widow's Mite: Luke 21:1-4

A mite was a small coin, worth almost nothing. Yet, in this story, when the widow gives her two mites—all she has—Jesus declares her gift greater than the much larger donations offered by those who are wealthy. This story reflects a modern reality: in the United States, many poor people give away a larger percentage of their income than those who have excess.[9]

> [Jesus] looked up and saw rich people putting their gifts into the treasury; he also saw a poor widow put in two small copper coins. He said, "Truly I tell you, this poor widow has put in more than all of them, for all of them have contributed out of their abundance, but she out of her poverty has put in all she had to live on."—Luke 21:1-4

This woman is presented as a hero, but the story isn't really about her. If it were, we would learn more. Does she always give all she has? What will she live on tomorrow? Where does she sleep? Does she have children who support her? How did she acquire those two coins? Is she embarrassed by her meager offering, or does she realize how much it means to give all she can?

The challenge when reading this story is to avoid romanticizing the widow as a model of the "noble poor"—those who remain quiet, self-deprecating, and never disturb the status quo. If we read her godly generosity as compliance, we could talk ourselves into

9. While those receiving direct cash assistance from the government give little, the working poor give, on average, about 12% of their income. While the gross amount that people give increases with income, the percentage declines. Middle-class and wealthy people only give around 3% of their income. There has been a trend in recent years for very wealthy people to give away a majority of their wealth, but this is not a general trend outside of this rarified air. See Philanthropy Round Table, *Statistics on U.S. Generosity,* Graph 11, philanthropyroundtable.org/almanac/statistics-on-u-s-generosity. Accessed October 11,2025.

believing that this is the role the poor should always occupy. I do not believe that Jesus wants anyone, especially the poor, to feel that they need to be quiet, to hide. The story's importance lies not in her modeling poverty, but in the stark contrast with the wealthy. Consider what Jesus said just a few verses earlier about some of the others present that day:

> In the hearing of all the people [Jesus] said to the disciples, "Beware of the scribes who like to walk around in long robes and who love respectful greetings in the marketplaces and the best seats in the synagogues and places of honor at banquets. They devour widows' houses and for the sake of appearance say long prayers. They will receive the greater condemnation."—Luke 20:45-47

These verses reveal that those who "devour widows' houses" are not thieves but so-called respectable citizens operating within the law. Wealthy and powerful, they use their excess to make loans to the needy, like desperate widows, then foreclose when payments cannot be met. The very people making a show of their generous gifts are responsible for the woman's poverty.

## Working Class

In the first congregation I served, one member, Lucy, put exactly one dollar each week in the collection plate. She had worked steadily from the moment she graduated high school, spending the last thirty years as a security guard downtown. Despite her decades of service, which earned her priority in scheduling and access to overtime shifts, she never received significant raises. After three decades, her base salary remained just over $20,000 per year.

Lucy never pledged, but if she missed a week (which was rare), she would put two dollars in the plate when she returned. This may well have been all that she could afford to give; nevertheless, when her granddaughter accompanied her, she would give the child a dollar for the plate in addition to her own. For Lucy, giving was essential to what it meant to be a Christian.

Lucy was part of what we typically call the "working class." This term refers primarily to those who perform manual labor. They might live in poverty or they might have incomes that could make them part of the middle class—the boundaries blur. However, no matter which income bracket they occupy, those who are poor and those who are working class face two distinct challenges within the culture of the United States. The first is external oppression: the assumptions people make and the systems they create that make it harder to get ahead.

The second challenge is internalized oppression—accepting these unfair assumptions as truth. I have a friend who insists that her difficult life, always one step away from homelessness, "is [her] own damned fault." Yes, she has made some mistakes in her life. But haven't we all? Should the consequences of making mistakes mean homelessness? Hunger for our children? Endless suffering? Internalized oppression prevents her from seeing the distinction: while her mistakes are, in fact, her fault, the system is stacked against her. Lucy is by all definitions a hard-working person with a full-time job, who volunteers regularly for overtime. And yet that pay is barely enough to keep up with the regular costs of housing, food, and healthcare.

## Oppression

Poverty intersects with many forms of oppression, particularly oppression based on gender, race, immigration status, and disability. Women face higher poverty rates due to low wages and the fact that they often become sole caregivers for children after a separation or divorce. Black Americans are disadvantaged by the lingering legacies of slavery, redlining, and other systemic exclusions that prevented the accumulation of generational wealth. Immigrants of all races face a baseline level of discrimination, Hispanic people, in particular, are often presumed to be immigrants, regardless of their citizenship status. Meanwhile, though our nation provides disability benefits, they are bafflingly set at poverty levels, likely out of fear that adequate support might encourage able-bodied people to try and exploit the system.

Consider my parishioner Joe, who needed surgery requiring three weeks of recovery. When he informed the grocery store where he worked about the surgery, they immediately laid him off. Joe misunderstood this as a permanent termination—he didn't realize he could return after recovering. Believing that he no longer had a job, he told his landlord he couldn't pay his rent and left his apartment voluntarily rather than taking advantage of the extended eviction process. When I discovered he was suddenly homeless two weeks before his scheduled surgery, he explained he was just trying to do what was right.

In our system, who exactly is supposed to help Joe?

## Classism

We use the term *classism* to describe the oppression of people based on their poverty. This oppression manifests through stereotypes, uneven application of rules, erasure of people's experiences, and even seemingly positive but ultimately harmful views like the idea of the "noble poor." In the United States, people commonly assume that people who are poor are uneducated, unwise, lazy, addicted, or unemployed. These stereotypes are simply not true! But even if they were, should there be such heavy social and material penalties for lacking education? For making unwise choices? For being unemployed? For not working hard enough?

Casual classism frequently shows up when people who are not poor explain their path to success. "I deserve what I have," they might say, or more commonly, "I worked hard to get where I am."

I always want to ask what they mean. What does "working hard' really look like? How does it compare to waiting tables for eight hours straight? To construction work? To days spent in a hot, loud kitchen that's constantly in motion? To lugging heavy items around a warehouse day after day after day?

While some people certainly work harder than others, it's simply false that those who work the hardest make the most money. I learned this firsthand when I worked at a local newspaper. I had a reputation for "working hard." I stayed late regularly, often taking a dinner break then heading back to the office. After ten years of this, I decided to set some boundaries and limited myself to no more than fifty hours per week. Surprisingly, I accomplished the same amount of work. I hadn't been working "hard"—I'd been working "long." Or perhaps more accurately, working slowly.

Poor people often juggle more than one job and work more than forty hours per week. Part-time workers often desperately want full-time positions. Those with irregular schedules struggle to add a second job, even when they need the income. My nephew works summer and winter jobs at the same facility, but the employer mandates unpaid breaks in the fall and spring—ensuring that my nephew and others like him remain classified as seasonal rather than permanent employees, thereby denying them benefits.

Classism operates systemically as well. Flat-fee fines—parking tickets, speeding tickets, late registration penalties, towing fees—can all be devastating for those dealing with poverty while barely affecting the more affluent. Does your "free" checking account require a minimum balance? That's quietly a tax for being too poor.

Even food access reveals systemic issues. The cheapest option for food—buying groceries and cooking at home—generally requires time, reliable transportation, and stable housing. Without cars, poor families are forced to depend on corner markets that charge higher prices, stock fewer choices, and rarely carry fresh produce. For someone balancing three jobs, picking up fast food between shifts may be the only option despite being the most expensive one. It's another recurring fee for living in poverty.

Consider how differently we treat government assistance for the poor versus assistance for the wealthy. When middle-class homeowners claim the mortgage interest deduction, what proof do they have to provide that the benefit is deserved? None. I just copy a number from my mortgage tax form onto my tax return. Personally, I receive an additional deduction for a failed real estate investment from several years ago. Each year, I enter the loss, carry forward the excess, and reduce my adjusted gross income. To claim this benefit, I merely fill in a box on the appropriate schedule. It works out great for me, but is it fair?

Now, contrast this with applying for benefits when you're poor. For SNAP benefits, you first start with an application, then a mandatory interview that requires taking time off from an hourly job. Each state maintains its own website with a list of required documentation that you have to provide or the whole process grinds to a halt. Besides basic information—name, Social Security number, proof of address—you must verify the wages of not only yourself but everyone who lives in your household. You might also choose to submit additional proof of housing costs, utilities, medical expenses, and childcare costs, but only if you believe that doing so will strengthen your case. This bureaucratic maze constitutes a time tax on those living in poverty.

## The Sheep and the Goats: Matthew 25:31-46

How will we be judged as Christians based on our response to poverty? What is our role and our responsibility when it comes to helping those carrying this burden? In Matthew 25:31-46, all nations gather before the king, who separates them into sheep at his right hand and goats at his left; then he proclaims judgment:

> Then the king will say to those at his right hand, 'Come, you who are blessed by my Father, inherit the kingdom prepared for you from the foundation of the world, for I was hungry and you gave me food, I was thirsty and you gave me something to drink, I was a stranger and you welcomed me, I was naked and you gave me clothing, I was sick and you took care of me, I was in prison and you visited me.' Then the righteous will answer him, 'Lord, when was it that we saw you hungry and gave you food or thirsty and gave you something to drink? And when was it that we saw you a stranger and welcomed you or naked and gave you clothing? And when was it that we saw you sick or in prison and visited you?' And the king will answer them, 'Truly I tell you, just as you did it to one of the least of these brothers and sisters of mine, you did it to me.'—Matthew 25:34-40

To everyone's surprise, the judgment rests entirely on care for those who are poor, strangers, sick, and in prison. There is no test of belief, lifestyle, or baptism. The second surprise is that these people in need *are* Jesus. Whatever we do for people in need, we do for Jesus himself. Note carefully that they are not *like* Jesus—they *are* Jesus. Taking this understanding and flipping it transforms our reading of the anointing story from Mark 14: the woman was, in fact, comforting the poor because Jesus *is* the poor.

## What Should We Do as Christians?

Christians are called to care for people in need. As individuals, we can easily give a few dollars to someone on the street, donate to charitable organizations, and volunteer our time. My friend Paul went so far as to convert some of his rental properties into affordable housing, building relationships with tenants who were struggling financially. Some of us create employment opportunities that empower those who are poor. Many of us provide financial support to family members when they're in need.

While we can certainly alleviate suffering to some extent with our individual actions, we can do so much more in community. As churches, we establish food pantries, meal programs, and clothing closets. We get to cook for those transitioning from prison, those in recovery, or those experiencing homelessness. As a community, we support immigrants in our churches and neighborhoods. We open our buildings for recovery programs, English-as-a-second-language classes, and daycare centers. We look out for members of our community who are struggling.

## Conclusion

Liberation theology suggests that God has a preferential option for people who are poor and working class. Jesus' words—the poor will always be with you, the story of the widow's mite, the story of the sheep and the goats—give us a view of how Christians engage with people who are poor. They are Christ to us; they are honorable; they are always present.

Rather than define poverty as a specific income, we are talking about people who don't have enough material resources for the basics of life: housing, food, healthcare, plus a little extra for emergencies. People are poor for many reasons, but classism and other forms of oppression make it hard to move out of poverty. The question of what constitutes material poverty is closely connected to our next topic: what is wealth?

## LENTEN REFLECTIONS

### A DAILY PRAYER FOR THE SECOND WEEK OF LENT

Holy one, help us to see you in people who are poor and working class. Help us to see you in people who are struggling. Help us to honor each person as someone made in your image, as your child, and as our sibling. Forgive us for the ways we do not share your wealth more equitably in our nation and in the world. Holy one, help us to see you in all whom we meet. Amen.

### SECOND WEEK OF LENT

#### MONDAY REFLECTIONS • Housing

Do you have adequate housing with a functional kitchen and sufficient heating and cooling? Does housing cost less than 30% of your income when you include utilities, insurance, and property taxes? If you are married, could you afford to stay where you live if you lost your spouse? What stories does your family tell about the house or land where you grew up? If your current housing is beyond your means, could you move somewhere more affordable within the next year? Within five years?

#### TUESDAY REFLECTIONS • Food and Drink

Do you and your children have reliable access to three meals a day and clean water? Can you regularly obtain fresh fruits and vegetables? If you qualify for SNAP (food stamps), food pantries, or meal programs, are you using these resources? Do you have time to cook and clean up afterward? What portion of your food budget goes to alcohol, restaurants, or fast food? Do you have the time and energy to prepare more meals at home? How does your relationship with food and your body affect you emotionally? What stories does your family tell about food or drink?

## WEDNESDAY REFLECTIONS • Benefits

Do you currently have a paying job? Do you have more than one? Two? Three? Do you provide unpaid care for someone? Would you prefer more paid work or less? What benefits does your employment provide: sick leave, paid vacation, personal time off? Do you have health insurance, retirement contributions, life and disability insurance, or health savings accounts? Is your health insurance adequate for your needs? Do you receive disability benefits through Supplemental Security Income (SSI) or Social Security Disability Insurance (SSDI)? If not, should you apply? Do you know how to navigate the application process? How do you feel about managing your physical or mental health challenges—is there guilt involved? What messages did your family pass down about handling illness and taking sick time?

## THURSDAY REFLECTIONS • Dependents

Who relies on your income? Who helps you with your expenses? Are you caring for parents or extended family members, or are they caring for you? Do you face significant costs for childcare, education, or supporting family members with disabilities? Does caregiving prevent you from pursuing paid work? Is your role caring for others working out the way you expected it would? If you are receiving care, is this situation functioning the way you anticipated? What emotions does this arrangement bring up: anger, guilt, frustration, or something else?

## FRIDAY REFLECTIONS • Savings and Debt

Are you saving money or accumulating debt? Will your retirement funds sustain you for as long as you need? If you have a partner, would the loss of your partner leave you in a financial crisis? Do you have a bank account in your own name? Could you access three months expenses in case of an emergency? Six months? What debts do you carry—mortgages, car loans, student loans? Are the payments for these manageable, given your income? Could you reduce the debt within the next year? What emotions do you feel regarding your debt? Guilt, frustration, shame? What stories did your family tell about borrowing and debt when you were growing up?

## SATURDAY REFLECTIONS • Time

Do you have time to take care of yourself and your family? What changes could you make to carve out more time in your life? Are you able to take vacations, or do you need a break you can't seem to take? Have you ever taken a mental health day from work? If so, how did you spend that time? Do you have a hobby that allows you to take a mental break from work? If it's expensive, does the cost prevent you from engaging with it more? Could you find ways to dedicate more time to activities that restore you like your hobby?

## SUNDAY REFLECTIONS • Celebrating What You Have

What financial accomplishments have you achieved that have made you proud? What creative solutions have you found to respond to a difficult financial problem? What aspect of your career or work history brings you satisfaction? Where have you encountered God in your financial journey? In what ways has God felt present during financial struggles? In what ways has God felt absent?

# INTERLUDE

## The Pastor's Discretionary Fund

While churches and organizations want to be responsible with their financial support, this sometimes leads to policies that create artificial limits. Dorothy, the church secretary at the congregation I served, was diligent and took her gatekeeping responsibility seriously—she didn't want the church to be taken advantage of. Yet this church also held millions in endowments and regularly budgeted for a modest pastor's discretionary fund.

When a woman called asking for help one day, I encouraged Dorothy to schedule an appointment. The woman arrived and immediately launched into her story, barely pausing for breath. When she finally ran out of steam, I asked what she needed: a $25 grocery card.

"Can I pray for you?" I offered.

"Oh no," she said, "I'm good. But will you pray for my daughter?"

So, we prayed for her daughter and her situation. I added in a prayer for the woman as well. Dorothy dutifully recorded the gift card distribution. After the woman left, Dorothy informed me that this was the second gift card the woman had received this month. Church policy limited recipients to no more than one.

"Are we running out?" I asked. I could always move money from the pastor's fund to buy more cards.

"No, we have plenty."

"I think it's fine. Let me know when we are starting to run low," I responded.

Honestly, discretionary funds are difficult to manage. It's not because I hate giving money away—honestly, I wish we could do more. The problem is that these funds reward people for telling compelling stories, or at least that's how those asking for help perceive it. People seeking help seem to try and calibrate their stories just right, striking a balance between apologetic confession and angelic intentions. Good stories get money, help, and prayers, while those with messier, more complicated, or less positive stories get turned away. It's a twisted series of incentives and seems far from what Jesus meant when he called us to do what we could to help the least of these.

Certainly, some who ask for help are dishonest, making the rounds to collect what they can from every available source. The challenge is to avoid becoming cynical when we inevitably give to the wrong person. Many churches keep detailed lists of who has asked for what and when. Others, like the church where I served, limit each person to one or two requests per year. But poverty doesn't work like that; it doesn't adhere to neat patterns. Some people need substantial help, while others need very little, and none of us know when we might be in need next.

# Wealth

## My Story

My husband and I didn't realize we were wealthy—or at least that we had excess—until we got serious about planning for retirement. Had I been paying attention, I would have noticed how much we spent on things that are not necessities. But it wasn't until we received an inheritance from Ken's dad that doubled our savings and started asking questions like "When can we retire?" that we discovered we were doing well.

Our definition of "wealth" is built upon three pillars: 1) owning a home, 2) bringing in an income that slightly exceeds our expenses, and 3) having enough money saved to retire. As I write this, we owe less than half of our home's current value on our mortgage, which we'll pay off right around the time we transition to retirement living. Between Social Security, required minimum distributions from our retirement savings, and my pension, our retirement income will roughly match what we earn now while we are both working.

We stumbled into this security rather than planned for it. Though our income is modest for Massachusetts, we live far enough outside of Boston to manage comfortably. Also, while we've both worked almost exclusively for nonprofits, I was able to build a decent retirement account during my years at a newspaper. Ken's income has grown slowly but steadily, while mine fluctuates.

Beyond that, I have a pension, while Ken's employer contributed to a 403(b) retirement plan.

We both were raised in families with conservative spending habits and have maintained those values in our own lives. Ken's parents always chose the cheapest option available—I remember his mom being upset when we took her to a sit-down restaurant for her birthday instead of Burger King, unable to enjoy what she saw as wasteful spending. Neither of us could maintain our lifestyle on a single income. While most of our neighbors earn more than we do and are savvier about savings and investments, we have what we need: food, healthcare, housing, plus enough for emergencies, vacations, and various hobbies. It helps that we don't have kids and don't face any of the expenses for childcare, clothing, school and activity fees, and eventual tuition costs.

By some measures, we've saved less than we should have and we've missed out on some opportunities to join savings programs at Ken's workplace because we simply weren't paying attention. For many people, such oversights would prove disastrous. For us, inherited generational wealth provided a cushion to absorb these mistakes and ensure we can retire comfortably. We might not be considered rich, but we are rich *enough*.

## What to Do About Our Wealth?

You may find it strange to hear someone talk so openly about their financial situation. Our culture has built up a certain taboo around openly discussing affluence. It's important to open the conversation this way because this chapter is not about how to handle poverty, but about what to do with wealth. Those of us who have excess must grapple with difficult questions: What should we do with what we have? How does our surplus distance us from God? Does our abundance lead us to genuine thankfulness for our blessings? Does it become a barrier to spiritual growth?

The gospel demands that we examine our wealth. We will probably not come to perfect conclusions, and I encourage readers to hold their views tentatively and ask how wealth affects their connection to God, to their neighbors, and to themselves. Keep these questions open and hold your answers lightly as we explore them throughout this book.

## Woe to Those with Wealth and Power: Luke 6:24-26

Luke offers little kindness to the wealthy. Many churches today downplay God's judgment, emphasizing love over anger—an approach I prefer in many ways. Talking more about God's love and less about God's anger feels good and affirming.

Yet the biblical witness includes a lot of judgment. Luke, in particular, presents a Jesus who condemns those with power and money. Jesus lived in an honor/shame society where wealth brought honor and poverty brought shame. However, Jesus sees this the other way around. The poor are the blessed, and woe to those who have wealth. (See also Luke 10:13-15, 11:42-43, and 17:1-4.)

> "But woe to you who are rich,
> for you have received your consolation.
> "Woe to you who are full now,
> for you will be hungry.
> "Woe to you who are laughing now,
> for you will mourn and weep.
>
> "Woe to you when all speak well of you, for that is how
> their ancestors treated the false prophets.
> —Luke 6:24-26

Luke writes in the present tense; this judgment is about the wealth we have right now. The blessing in Luke 6:20—"Blessed are you who are poor for yours is the kingdom of God"—promises a future reversal, as does the corresponding woe in verse 24. The rich have already received what they've been promised; the kingdom belongs to those who lack riches now. Those who feast today will be hungry; those who laugh will mourn.

For those of us who have plenty, this text raises an uncomfortable question: Do we really want the kingdom of God if it means giving up everything we have now to receive it?

## The Rich Man: Mark 10:17-22

When someone asked Jesus how to inherit eternal life, his first response is simple: follow God's commandments. It's straightforward: just do what is right. The rich man who asked the question claims to have done this throughout his life, yet pushes further and asks what else he should do:

> As he was setting out on a journey, a man ran up and knelt before him and asked him, "Good Teacher, what must I do to inherit eternal life?" Jesus said to him, "Why do you call me good? No one is good but God alone. You know the commandments: 'You shall not murder. You shall not commit adultery. You shall not steal. You shall not bear false witness. You shall not defraud. Honor your father and mother.'" He said to him, "Teacher, I have kept all these since my youth." Jesus, looking at him, loved him and said, "You lack one thing; go, sell what you own, and give the money to the poor, and you will have treasure in heaven; then come, follow me." When he heard this, he was shocked and went away grieving, for he had many possessions. —Mark 10:17-22

Mark says that Jesus loves this man. He engages him compassionately, trusts what he says, and recognizes his worthy life. Most significantly, Jesus invites the man to join his disciples! This is not an invitation extended casually or to everyone he meets. In contrast,

Zacchaeus (Luke 19:1-10) does not receive this invitation, Jesus doesn't even ask him to give up his job, just to stop cheating.

This righteous man seeks out the ultimate requirement, the one extraordinary act that will secure eternal life. When he hears what Jesus has to say, that he must give up his possessions, he is sad. I'm sad when I hear this too. Is Jesus truly calling all of us to sell all of our possessions, give everything to the poor, and follow him? That's certainly one way to read this story. Yet very, very few Christians choose this path. Most of us, myself included, don't give away everything we own. I'll be honest: I don't want to preach that this is what we are called to do because I don't want to do it myself.

Perhaps wealth's most insidious effect is that it makes us fear change and prevents us from desiring a better future. When I have plenty and things are good for me, any change in the status quo is a threat rather than an opportunity. The rich man's wealth—like my own—obscures the possibility that life with Jesus could be incomparably wonderful, far better than anything he has now. Jesus offers nothing less than a new identity to those who accept his radical invitation.

The most common interpretation of this story suggests that our attachment to things keeps us from fully following Jesus. The solution seems simple: consider your attachments and let them go. Perhaps this man was too attached to his money or his home or something else entirely. In this understanding of the story, the point is not necessarily to let go of our belongings, but to sever our unhealthy attachment to our belongings.

Another way to approach this challenging story is to choose to be like Zacchaeus instead. He invites Jesus to dinner, and when confronted by neighbors about his sins, he offers to give half his possessions to the poor and to repay any fraud four times over. Yet even this compromise troubles me. I don't want to give away half of my excess, either. Is there no other way to follow Jesus and do what's right?

> Then Jesus looked around and said to his disciples, "How hard it will be for those who have wealth to enter the kingdom of God!" And the disciples were perplexed at these words. But Jesus said to them again, "Children, how hard it is to enter the kingdom of God! It is easier for a camel to go through the eye of a needle than for someone who is rich to enter the kingdom of God." They were greatly astounded and said to one another, "Then who can be saved?" Jesus looked at them and said, "For mortals it is impossible, but not for God; for God all things are possible."—Mark 10:23-27

This story ends with Peter eagerly reminding Jesus that his disciples have given up everything to follow him. I've always assumed this sacrifice was easier for a poor fisherman like Peter than it would be for me—until I remember that Matthew was a tax collector and likely had significant wealth! Jesus acknowledges the near impossibility of the rich entering the kingdom of God on their own merit. But he also adds that with God all things are possible. It's a story that strikes a nerve at my core, but at least I have that to hold onto.

## Middle Class

One of the challenges with discussing poverty and wealth from a biblical perspective is that scripture typically portrays life at the extremes. Poor Lazarus lies covered in sores, a beggar abandoned at the gate. The widow possesses only two small coins. At the opposite end, King Solomon symbolizes the idea of wealth and affluence that has been given to him by God. He has more than enough of everything. In Jesus' time, the vast majority lived as destitute day laborers. A small group, like Jesus' father Joseph, worked as craftsmen, and an even smaller elite controlled almost all the wealth and power. Scripture rarely speaks directly about those of us living in the middle.

The most convenient response to scriptures on wealth is simple denial, to argue that they don't apply to me because I'm not wealthy. Or at least, I'm not *really* wealthy; I'm middle class. This is irrefutably true. I am neither poor nor, by conventional standards, wealthy. Yet, nearly everyone claims to be middle class, making us all ordinary people living ordinary lives. Identifying as middle class also ensures that we don't have to identify ourselves with "the poor" and therefore don't share their struggles as our own.

The numbers tell a more complex story. In 2022, the top 5% of U.S. households earned more than $295,000 annually, while the top 1% made at least $800,000 per year. These are undeniably the wealthy.

But where does the middle class actually fall? Some define it as household earnings between $40,000 and $130,000. One "middle-class" tax proposal included all households making up to $250,000 annually. Another source set the floor for the middle class at $80,000, which would classify half the nation as poor. Using the quintile system we discussed earlier, the middle fifth of Americans—the statistical middle of the middle class—earned between $58,000 and $94,000 with an average of $74,730 in annual income.[10]

But perhaps straight-up dollar amounts are not the best way to define these terms. In the previous chapter, I defined poverty as instability—lacking adequate housing, food, and healthcare, without resources to handle emergencies. In parallel, we might define wealth as stability plus excess—sufficient income for necessities, a safe place to live, decent healthcare, retirement savings, and money beyond these basics as well. I believe there is a gospel imperative to examine what it means to have wealth and what to do with our excess.

---

10. Briana Sullivan, Donald Hays, and Neil Bennett, "Wealth by Race of Householder," *Tax Policy Center Urban Institute & Brookings Institution*, April 23, 2024, https://taxpolicycenter.org/sites/default/files/statistics/images/income_quintiles_5.png. Accessed January 19, 2025.

The truth is that some of us are rich, even if we avoid the word. Throughout most of my life, my family has enjoyed steady access to food and housing with plenty of leisure time besides—all clear markers of wealth.

Meanwhile, two of my friends have rarely if ever escaped economic fragility. Despite sometimes earning large salaries, they remain trapped by debt, housing costs, medical expenses, and the crushing anxiety of living without family support or the resources to back them up in an emergency. This is their constant reality.

Yet I must also acknowledge that some financial struggles come from overspending rather than something more systemic. This is not intended as a judgment on others. The questions raised in this book are questions I'm asking myself as well. This Lent, as we explore the connection between our wealth and our faith, I challenge you to ask the question I must ask myself: What material things stand between me and God?

## Storing Wealth: Luke 12:16-21

Many people don't feel wealthy even if they have a comfortable income because of a modern source of anxiety that doesn't come up in the Bible: retirement. Today, the average person lives years, if not decades, beyond the end of their working years leading to fears that Social Security and whatever savings they have will either be insufficient or disappear entirely. Beyond day-to-day expenses, rising healthcare costs threaten bankruptcy. Also, we don't want to just survive through these last years; we want to do something! We want to travel, pursue hobbies, or simply spoil our grandchildren. We desperately want to save *enough*. We want to be safe.

This brings us to the parable of the barn-builder. When a rich man's land produces unexpected abundance, he faces a dilemma about what to do with this excess. His solution is to build more storage space, securing his comfort for the days ahead:

> Then [Jesus] told them a parable: "The land of a rich man produced abundantly. And he thought to himself, 'What should I do, for I have no place to store my crops?' Then he said, 'I will do this: I will pull down my barns and build larger ones, and there I will store all my grain and my goods. And I will say to my soul, Soul, you have ample goods laid up for many years; relax, eat, drink, be merry.' But God said to him, 'You fool! This very night your life is being demanded of you. And the things you have prepared, whose will they be?' So it is with those who store up treasures for themselves but are not rich toward God."—Luke 12:16-21

Instead of the comfortable, relaxing life he envisioned, the barn-builder completes the project and immediately dies. As the saying goes, "You can't take it with you." Jesus explains that this is what happens when you hoard treasures for yourself rather than "being rich toward God."

In the first-century, the wealthy comprised a tiny percentage of the population, yet had power in both the economy and the government. In contrast to the barn-builder, wealthy landowners and business owners were culturally obligated to hire a large number of laborers every day, to leave some extra crops in their fields to be harvested and taken home by the poorest in the community, and to support priests and rulers. In the Roman Empire of Jesus' time, accumulating wealth for the sake of wealth, storing wealth, was viewed as theft.[11]

Of course, storage barns are essential to agricultural life. Even subsistence farmers must preserve their harvest, keeping enough to eat through the year and seeds for next season's planting. This parable isn't about normal saving but about hoarding excess.

---

11. Bruce J. Marina and Richard L. Rohrbaugh, *Social Science Commentary on the Synoptic Gospels* (Minneapolis: Fortress Press, 1992), 48.

When I read this, I think about the inheritance my husband and I received when his dad died. We immediately opened new accounts to store this unexpected bounty. We already have Social Security and a pension; now we have this additional cushion. We save it not in order to eat, drink, and be merry, but to quiet our fears about the future.

Yet the barn-builder died right after finishing his storage. What if he hadn't died? How could anyone retire without storing some of their excess in bigger barns? Should we literally be like the lilies of the field and stop worrying about retirement? I'll be honest: that's a hard one for me; I worry constantly about retirement. Is saving for retirement the right thing, or are we the barn-builders?

The Bible offers another barn-building story in Genesis 41:28-36. Joseph interprets Pharaoh's dream, predicting seven good years followed by seven years of famine. He follows this up by saving the Egyptian people and building huge storehouses to save the excess produced during the good years. In this story, saving for the future is clearly the right thing to do.

But in Joseph's story, the barns serve a fundamentally different purpose. They aren't built for individual comfort—no eating, drinking, and being merry. Instead, the bigger barns represent how the kingdom cares for the entire community—collecting surplus during the good years to sustain everyone through the lean ones.

Jesus closes this parable by commanding us to "be rich toward God." Perhaps we do this by caring for God's people—the poor, the oppressed, the stranger, the widow, and the orphan. Instead of clinging to excess to protect us, we hold onto God.

## How to Become Wealthy

The mechanics of wealth are simple: when the amount you bring in is more than the amount you spend—whether from work or investments—wealth accumulates. You don't need to make a lot of money if you manage expenses carefully and avoid catastrophes.

It's also important to say that making money is not wrong. However, we must ask ourselves *how* we are making money. Does the work we do hurt or help the world? Do our investments encourage positive change and a healthy society? Does our employer treat us well but only at the expense of harming others? Do they pay living wages to their lowest-paid employees, or do they rely on government programs to pick up the rest of the tab?

While considering what is "good for the world" can be subjective, take time to consider your own values as well. Can you feel proud, as a Christian, of what you do for work? If not, what would it take to change direction and consider doing something different? Remember that those who are poor rarely have the luxury to choose where to work; people with excess have more options and therefore more responsibility.

Excess money also builds wealth through compound interest. During my decade in sales, I invested a significant amount of my surplus income. That account has grown to roughly three times its original size. Where did that extra money come from? I definitely didn't have to work for it—having money simply made me more money. My financial planner tries to normalizes things by calling this my "travel fund." I recognize it for what it is: my new, bigger barn. I'm storing wealth, just like the barn-builder from the parable.

The easiest path to wealth is to be born into it. Wealthy parents, or maybe some other wealthy family members, simply pass their wealth down to you. Eventually, you pass that wealth on to your own children. For most families, this kind of wealth builds slowly and varies significantly based on family circumstances. When I was in high school, my grandmother died and left us a little money. We used it to get a ping-pong table. On the other hand, when Ken's father died, we acquired a trailer, a tow vehicle, and doubled our retirement funds. His lifetime of careful investing paid off and was passed on to us.

Generational wealth also magnifies historical oppression. Consider the post-World War II GI Bill, which offered low-interest home loans to returning soldiers. Through redlining, these loans were systematically denied for housing in Black or integrated neighborhoods. White veterans received loans, bought houses, and built equity. Black and Brown veterans, on the other hand, did not. The resulting home ownership slowly created wealth that has now passed on to their children and grandchildren. This and other systemic discrimination helps to partially explain why white household wealth is ten times that of Black households—a much larger disparity than income would make it appear.[12]

## Why It's Okay to Be Wealthy

There's no simple answer to the question of what Christians should do with their wealth. Or rather, the simple answer is that we should give it all away . . . and we just don't want to. At least, *I* don't want to.

We might invoke God's blessing of King Solomon with wisdom and wealth (and wives) to explain our rationale. The prosperity gospel would argue that our material excess signals God's favor and that we are being blessed in anticipation for our eternal life with God.

Alternatively, we can argue that middle-class status means we aren't wealthy and exempts us from biblical statements about wealth. There just aren't any scriptures addressing our present context. Similarly, we might spiritualize the issue, arguing that Jesus' critique of wealth is not about wealth itself but is really about focusing on money rather than God. As long as we know that our treasure is in

12. Briana Sullivan, Donald Hays, and Neil Bennett, "Wealth by Race of Householder," Tax Policy Center Urban Institute & Brookings Institution, April 23, 2024, https://taxpolicycenter.org/sites/default/files/statistics/images/income_quintiles_5.png.

heaven, perhaps our earthly excess is irrelevant. Perhaps the issue isn't wealth itself but oppressive wealth. If we work for ethical businesses, do not take advantage of others, and actively work to improve the way we care for those who are poor, maybe that will mean we are good with God.

Or maybe we aren't *all* meant to follow Jesus' example fully. The rich young man is invited to give up everything and follow Jesus, while Zacchaeus—who is also wealthy—is neither invited to join the disciples nor asked to give away nearly as much. Can I choose to be a "pretty good" follower who keeps some of my wealth while others pursue a higher calling? Does God assign different responsibilities for different levels of faith?

Or perhaps wealth becomes something good as long as we share it generously. Having savings enables us to support and subsidize others, fund charitable organizations, and finance changes to the systems that are responsible for poverty. Giving money to organizations that help people who are poor—while also dealing with connected issues like immigration, disability, racism, sexism, and so forth—creates a net gain for the world. My concern with this argument (which I use myself!) is the follow-through. Are we *actually* giving that much away? I can't claim this defense while hoarding money in my big new barns. I can't say this and then perpetuate inequality by passing my excess on to family members who don't need it.

Perhaps our biblical calling is to keep only enough for a comfortable but not extravagant life, giving away everything beyond what's necessary for our essential needs. Of course, "essential" remains subjective. What does it mean to be comfortable as opposed to extravagant? More importantly, am I willing to examine which parts of my excess are keeping me from being closer to God?

## Money Is Meant to Be Spent

The barn-builder's problem wasn't earning excess but *storing* it. He was expected to spend his bounty and circulate it through the economy. Spending transfers wealth to others, supporting both individual recipients and, when done locally, entire communities. You receive goods or services while sellers receive a profit. Spending creates work. What we have come to call "trickle-down economics" presumes that the people who have the most money will also spend the most, thereby creating jobs.

I reject this theory for one simple reason: the wealthiest people spend only a small fraction of their income. Those in poverty spend every dollar—100 percent of income goes right back out. Most middle-class households aren't far behind, spending most of what they earn. While we can dismiss the theory that the spending of the wealthy creates jobs, we should still recognize that spending our own excess locally can benefit our neighbors.

Going out to dinner in my own community means I can tip service workers directly, making a direct impact on their income. When I hire a housekeeper, shop at local craft stores, or buy from the specialty cheese shop, my money goes straight to small business owners who will hopefully recirculate it themselves. The goal is to spend in ways where the recipients are likely to spend what I give them and continue moving money through our community. This is intended to speed up the "velocity of money." It's based on a theory that a dollar spent locally is then spent again and again, benefiting an ever-widening circle of people. It requires choosing businesses that will spend, not save, your dollar. To genuinely help those in poverty, we also should do our best to patronize businesses that share their earnings with their employees through better wages and benefits, particularly for their lowest-paid workers.

## Church Wealth

Wealth is not only about individuals. Churches have also built their own barns to store their excess. Consider all the possible ways churches set aside financial reserves: endowments, investment funds, named funds, restricted funds, and rainy-day accounts. Money that's been set aside for an unknown future is why many churches are still alive today. Many of these are memorial gifts and bequests that are designated for specific uses like Sunday school, choir, or building maintenance. These investments regularly "make" money on the stock market, as the church waits to disperse them.

Churches, especially large churches, typically spend only the returns on these investments, although, for decades, we saved even the returns for a rainy day. One church I serve has more than $10,000 set aside solely for flowers! Endowments provide churches with security, yet also reveal stark disparities. According to Adam Hearlson, one third of churches maintain endowments that provide additional operating income, and thus some stability to the church budget. These are also predominantly older, white congregations. In contrast, only one in twenty black congregations have these resources available to support them.[13]

Many of these churches still guard these reserves zealously, even as congregational membership dwindles. As churches close, we must ask ourselves an urgent question: What is this money actually for? I want to shout: "It's raining! The rainy day is here!" Now is the time to spend this money, and I hope that some of it, most of it, will go to create alternative forms of church that may never become self-sustaining—street churches, wild churches,

13. Adam Hearlson, "What Is a Church's Money For?," *The Christian Century*, August 2024, https://www.christiancentury.org/features/what-church-s-money, 69.

dinner churches and more, intended primarily to serve people who are poor, lonely, or lost.[14]

I believe the test for the use of church investment funds is simple: Is this actively helping to spread the good news, or is it being saved for a future that may never come? If we can somehow figure out how to use what we have saved to help our community, then perhaps it is right to have saved this money.

## What Can We Do?

Reimagining your church's wealth as a present resource rather than future insurance requires a fundamental shift in thinking. Your congregation will need to have honest conversations to come to terms with this new approach. Yes, it will feel frightening—these funds have long served as a safety net. Yet as a nonprofit, you're legally required to use funds to carry out your mission. Surely a church's mission includes caring for those who are poor and oppressed.

The first step is to identify who needs help in your community, then determine how to distribute your savings to serve them. What if your church covered the cost for hearing aids and eyeglasses? What if the church paid for gasoline for anyone struggling financially? What if your church provided staples—bread, eggs, and milk—to everyone who walked through your doors? What if you just handed each visitor $25 or distributed new shoes annually? What would this radical generosity say about who we are as a church?

Not every idea has to be focused on individuals either. A white church with a large endowment could share its wealth with a neighboring Black church. It could also fund health insurance for pastors at new church starts. Or all the churches in a region could

14. Street churches serve people who live on the streets and those at risk of homelessness. Most meet outside. Wild churches also meet outdoors, often on hiking trails or state parks. Dinner churches gather around a shared meal.

collaborate and determine specific missions for each congregation, then allocate their investment funds to each church based on what it needs to carry out that particular mission. Surely, we can imagine ways that God wants us to use these funds for the community rather than letting them sit idle in big barns.

As individuals, we face the same question: What do we do with our current excess and with the wealth we'll leave behind? The biggest issue to consider is the role you want to play in passing on generational wealth (if you have it). Once you have saved enough for retirement, perhaps it's time to give away more of your excess. Earlier in life, you will naturally focus more on protecting your spouse and children and providing a stable future for them. Additionally, if you support someone with disabilities, you must save for their ongoing care.

However, once family members are grown and making it on their own, we must seriously consider whether it is right to pass on generational wealth to people who are already stable. Now is the time to identify organizations and individuals who need our resources more than our immediate family needs them. If all goes well and our health holds, Ken and I will leave behind nearly a million dollars when we die. (I know it can be awkward to share financial details like this, but part of dealing with wealth is refusing to hide it behind a curtain of silence.) While I'd like to leave something to younger family members, they're already well-established on their own. My money would almost certainly make more of a difference in the world if I give it to organizations or churches that are helping people who are poor.

## Conclusion

By defining wealth as synonymous with excess, we identify the middle class as included in Jesus' admonitions against wealth. We look at the biblical stories and see that the wealthy are facing woe, are told to give all that they have away, and are warned not to store their excess for an unknown future. Both churches and individuals are called to distribute what they have stored. We do that by spending—preferably in ways that spread our resources to people who are poor—and by giving money away.

All of us, the poor and the wealthy alike, are encouraged to find our way closer to God. Next, we will explore what *spiritual* poverty is all about.

## LENTEN REFLECTIONS

### A DAILY PRAYER FOR THE THIRD WEEK OF LENT

Holy one, help us to see you in those who are wealthy. Help us to see our own wealth and guide us in our struggle to handle our excess faithfully. Forgive us for the ways we worry and how we hoard and hold on to what is yours alone. Holy one, help us to see you in all whom we meet. Amen.

### THIRD WEEK OF LENT

#### MONDAY REFLECTIONS • Income

How much money do you earn as an individual each month? How much does your household bring in? Do you provide unpaid labor that keeps your household functioning? If so, how do you value that contribution? How does your income compare to the national and local median income? How does this shape the way you see your financial status in context?

Does your work provide you with a way to serve others and meet their needs? Do you find it satisfying? Does it pay enough to cover your expenses? Can you take pride in your employer's mission and practices? Do you feel good about what you do? Is your work sustainable for your physical and mental health?

#### TUESDAY REFLECTIONS • Family

Are you currently able to provide for the needs of your family at a comfortable level? Do your children require specialized programs or additional support that is necessary for their well-being? If so, are you able to afford that? Are you responsible for supporting extended family? If so, does this support align with your values and your financial situation? If not, would it be possible to support your extended family? Are any of your extended family in need of support?

## WEDNESDAY REFLECTIONS • Things

Does housing constitute a reasonable portion of your income? If not, are there ways to remedy that in the near to medium-term future? Do you and your family have adequate clothing? Can you afford food that is both nutritious and delicious? Do you have access to this kind of food? Is there enough of it? Do you have the tools necessary to maintain your home? Can you afford to do activities that bring you joy, like hobbies or taking vacations?

## THURSDAY REFLECTIONS • Investments and Retirement

Are you saving enough for retirement, or does the amount feel insufficient? What concerns do you have about healthcare and housing in your later years? Do you plan to keep working once you retire? Do you want to? Is your current work kind to your body? If not, how will this affect you later and are you prepared for this possibility? How much of your income comes from investment? Where did the money you've invested come from? Is this the best use of your money currently?

## FRIDAY REFLECTIONS • Generational Wealth

Have you inherited any family wealth? Do you expect to receive any inheritance in the future? Are you planning to leave wealth to your own family? If so, do they genuinely need that wealth? Have you created or updated your will recently? What other actions are you taking to designate where your money should go after you die? Have you thought about what organizations can use your wealth? What issues and organizations are you passionate about that you could support this way?

## SATURDAY REFLECTIONS • Excess

Do you have more money coming in than going out? Are you accumulating savings beyond what you will need for your retirement years? Does anxiety about the future drive your financial decisions and your choices about savings? Do you use "retail therapy" as emotional comfort? Do you have more material things than you need? Are there patterns of hoarding in your family history?

Consider these possible changes: Would it make sense to live in a smaller home or a less expensive area? Would it make sense to buy fewer new clothes or to buy clothes from thrift stores?

## SUNDAY REFLECTIONS • Celebrating Achievements

What accomplishments bring you the most pride today? Are there times when you have made difficult choices or taken a harder path that paid off for you in the long run? Think about the pivotal decisions you've made in your life. What is the story you tell about choosing your career, your spouse, or where you live that has shaped you? How do these stories shape the way you view yourself and your position in life?

# INTERLUDE

## Disrupting Pay Day Lending: Two Approaches

One of my dreams about how to help the poor is for churches to create banks, lending organizations, or something that actually puts money in the hands of people who need it. I was delighted to discover two examples of this.

Shirley Bondon, a lawyer, serves as executive director of the Black Clergy Collaborative of Memphis. This coalition of thirty to forty churches works to do whatever is necessary to respond to poverty in their community. They've established farmers' markets, promoted civic engagement, created juvenile justice diversion programs, advanced health equity, and more. However, their work creating an alternative to payday lending particularly caught my attention.

Payday lenders are everywhere in impoverished areas. These lenders provide small loans to the working poor so that they can cover the gap between today, when a payment is due, and next week, when their paycheck arrives. These loans are incredibly exploitative, carrying exorbitant fees and high interest rates. In his book *Poverty by America*, Matthew Desmond reports that a loan for $375 rolled over a few times, as commonly happens, could accumulate $520 in fees within five months.[15] Traditional banks avoid offering such small loans, not because they're risky, but because the cost of doing the paperwork could exceed any potential return.

However, these loans do fill a painful gap in our financial system. In Worcester, Massachusetts, I knew people who relied on payday loans for medical bills, car repairs, and to fix damage to their

15. Matthew Desmond, *Poverty By America* (New York: Crown, 2023), 76.

apartment. While all payday borrowers are employed, those living paycheck to paycheck simply cannot afford to repay the full loan amount when it comes due—typically within a week. Though the interest seems manageable if repaid immediately, few borrowers can manage to make that quick turnaround work.

In Memphis, forty percent of residents do not have a credit card, so payday lenders play a substantial role in providing short-term loans. The Black Clergy Collaborative wanted to create an alternative and partnered with Hope Credit Union to create another option. Since most banks are unwilling to provide a payday program due to the administrative costs, the collaborative worked with the credit union to make it more viable. The collaborative provides $50,000 as a security for the loans, while the credit union handles the administration and distribution. These loans run from $500 to $1,000 dollars with six-month to one-year terms. The money is distributed in two installments and can be used to cover essential expenses like car repairs, rent, insurance payments, and so forth.

Because the borrowers work with a credit union, they also end up with a checking account and begin to build their credit history by paying back the loan. The borrowers, most of whom are members of local churches, can also apply through their local congregation, making the process easier and more accessible.

A similar organization, Exodus Lending, started up at Holy Trinity Lutheran Church in South Minneapolis, Minnesota, in 2011, and has now been spun off as its own nonprofit. This community-organizing congregation wondered why there were so many payday lenders operating in their neighborhood. For ten years, the congregation worked to end the practice of predatory lending in Minnesota, but as they continued to learn about the industry, they discovered an uncomfortable truth: people in low-income neighborhoods genuinely needed these services. Where else can someone go when they have an emergency expense, but have no credit card, bank account, or family with extra cash?

Holy Trinity responded by offering to refinance payday loans out of the church office. Their initial plan was simple. They raised $10,000 and began refinancing small loans interest free. To date, they have a ninety percent repayment rate. Those who want to invest in this program are asked to provide $10,000 for three years, which is then returned to them without interest. In addition, Holy Trinity raises funds to cover shortages stemming from loans that are not repaid.

The loans offered by Exodus Lending are each limited to $1,500, although many borrowers have multiple loans. Once one loan is paid down, users can get additional loans. Exodus uses a "high-touch" strategy with borrowers, spending much of their time explaining terms, setting up ways for people to defer payments, and referring users to financial counseling and other services to provide them with more holistic support. The program's largest expense is their staff, but they've become attractive to funders, and in 2024, they received a large grant to expand their work statewide.

While Exodus Lending was initially concerned that their church connections might deter people from working with them, it turned out that this was exactly what people needed to understand that a lender offering zero percent interest was not a scam! Program participants also requested that Exodus report their repayments to credit bureaus as a way to help build their credit scores and repair their credit history. In 2019, Exodus Lending was able to start doing that.

There's an interesting lesson to be learned from these payday lending alternatives. Many of the borrowers did not need education about budgeting or lending. They knew exactly what was going on with these predatory loans. The problem was that there wasn't another choice for dealing with emergencies.

Every neighborhood in every city should have a church working to address the exorbitant rates that people face from payday lenders. We need to take action politically to make it illegal to charge such high rates, but also locally to provide simple, straightforward alternative lending sources for people facing emergencies.

4

# Spiritual Poverty

## My Story

As taboo as the topic is, I find it easier to talk about my money and wealth than to talk about my spiritual poverty. Talking about spiritual poverty—this whole relationship-to-God thing, this stuff about seeking God, this faith that requires me to be vulnerable—really makes me uncomfortable. I'm a doer by nature, but spiritual poverty concerns itself more with how one chooses to *be* than what one chooses to *do*.

My instinct during hard times is to make a list of all the things I can do right now to fix it. It's how I respond to problems in our society, in my community, and in my life. But spiritual poverty requires something else; it requires humility. It requires the humility to acknowledge that I can't fix it, and this recognition leaves me dependent on God. It leads me to turn to God for refuge during times of trouble rather than relying on my own efforts.

The two hardest times of my life were my spouse's death and, later, my seventeen-year-old niece's death. Looking back, God was very near to me during both crises. I responded to that divine closeness by lashing out in anger and despair. When dealing with my day-to-day frustrations about the world and how God's work unfolds within it, I tend to try and set God aside, dismissing God's role as almost irrelevant. I operate from a simple theology: God created us;

we screwed up, and now it's my job to try and figure out how to help humanity do better. But when crisis comes, when death arrives, God is not easily dismissed.

Perhaps if I were more humble, I would have allowed myself to feel God's care for me. What I understand now, having found life again, is that God was always nearby. Honestly, God was suffocatingly close, but I craved the opposite. I wanted to be free from all attachments, free from family who kept offering useful things to read, free from friends who extended kindness and concern, and free from God's offer of refuge. I wanted to focus only on how God had failed to save me from pain. That's what I wanted, and it would have been so bad for me.

I am astounded by God's ability to continue being loving and present when all I offered was disdain. Every word I spoke came out as anger. I refused every opportunity for comfort or relief. I was determined to remain as miserable as possible for as long as possible.

Then, one day, years later, something shifted. For each of these impossible experiences of grief, a day finally came when I released my anger. In a single moment, the unbearable became bearable. Everything that happened remained awful, but I could live with it. In those moments of release, I let go of my illusion of control. I surrendered the belief that I was in charge or that I was the one who had to make it right. I abandoned the belief that I should, or even could, fix it all. I learned, again and again, that dependence is not weakness but the fundamental human condition.

I realized that God is bigger than I am and that I am loved and accepted exactly as I am. I found humility, at least for a while. It is truly humbling to be loved as I am and not as I want myself to be.

## The Essentials of Spiritual Poverty

Spiritual poverty is about who we are as individuals. It is a positive quality that brings us closer to God. Some biblical interpretations mistakenly suggest that material poverty brings about spiritual poverty, or worse, that being poor is good because it brings a person closer to God. While humility may come easier to those who do not have wealth, this does not make material poverty desirable or good.

Spiritual poverty involves humility—the ability to remain open to divine guidance while recognizing our profound dependence on God. The prophets suggest that there are few who are truly spiritually poor; they are the faithful remnant who, facing destruction, choose to care for the poor and oppressed rather than seek power. In Zephaniah 3:12-13, God promises to preserve such a remnant: "For I will leave in the midst of you a people humble and lowly. They shall seek refuge in the name of the LORD—the remnant of Israel." This remnant trusts God and lives out God's laws, even in difficult times.

Lent invites us to step back, breathe deeply, and cultivate spiritual poverty. During this season, we examine ourselves honestly, focusing on our need for God. This Lent, I invite you to identify what keeps you from embracing this dependence.

## Internalized Oppression

What appears to be humility can sometimes mask internalized oppression. This occurs when people facing oppression—whether due to poverty, race, gender, immigration status, or education—begin to believe they are inherently worth less than those who oppress them. They fall prey to the message offered by the oppressive powers and accept it as truth.

I see this frequently among people living in poverty. My friends will list all the things they've done and mistakes they've made that they believe have led to their difficult circumstances. And yes, they have made mistakes—but I've made similar mistakes while backed up by more family support. The difference between their poverty and my stability isn't the number of mistakes they've made but the lack of safety nets to catch them afterward. The true cause of poverty almost always lies beyond the control of a single person. Instead, it can be traced to a medical emergency, a loved one's death or long sickness, a natural disaster, or the violence and chaos in an immigrant's home country that forced their departure. Often, it's a mix of all the above.

Notice the contrasting narrative of those who are wealthy and those who are poor. Many people with excess talk about what they've done right to get where they are. People who are poor talk about what they've done wrong. Internalized oppression reduces people to their failures if they're poor and insists on their achievements if they're wealthy. Neither narrative tells the whole truth.

Spiritual poverty doesn't require self-deprecation or identifying yourself as sinful. We are all good enough for God. We are all worthy of God's love. Instead, spiritual poverty means recognizing that God is present—with you, with me, with us—helping us through both our successes and our failures. Perhaps we can say that spiritual poverty calls the haughty to be humble while calling those who diminish themselves to recognize their own worth.

## The Blessed

Matthew's Beatitudes offer the most direct reference to spiritual poverty in scripture. Scholars generally view this list of blessings as a single package, rather than individual blessings for separate virtues. The poor in spirit are also those who mourn, the meek, those who hunger and thirst for righteousness, the merciful, the pure in heart, and the peacemakers.

> "Blessed are the poor in spirit, for theirs is the kingdom of heaven.
> "Blessed are those who mourn, for they will be comforted.
> "Blessed are the meek, for they will inherit the earth.
> "Blessed are those who hunger and thirst for righteousness, for they will be filled.
> "Blessed are the merciful, for they will receive mercy.

"Blessed are the pure in heart, for they will see God.
"Blessed are the peacemakers, for they will be called
children of God.
"Blessed are those who are persecuted for the sake of
righteousness, for theirs is the kingdom of heaven.
—Matthew 5:3-10

Some interpret Matthew's "poor in spirit" to include both those suffering from material poverty and those with spiritual humility. However, we must avoid the trap of assuming that material poverty itself counts as a blessing. Eugene Boring, writing in the *New Interpreter's Bible*, reads this to say that the blessing is on the community rather than individuals.[16] The point is not that being destitute is blessed, but that communities that do not accumulate wealth demonstrate their dependence on God. Individuals who prioritize the community over their own personal resources embody this dependence as well.

## What Is Dependence on God?

When I learned to pray, I was taught to pray for God to take care of me—to protect me from disasters, famines, death, and serious illness. Yet I've learned that depending on God does not shield us from these terrible realities. I simply refuse to believe that God intentionally ignored the cries during the Holocaust, Stalin's purges, the Rwandan genocide, or the more intimate suffering of those contemplating suicide or weeping over the bed of a child with cancer. A loving God would not allow families to lose children or allow people to suffer from indiscriminate violence if divine intervention were a possibility. I've concluded that God doesn't interfere with the natural consequences of human choices or redirect natural disasters.

16. Eugene Boring, "The Gospel of Matthew," in Leader Keck et al., ed., *The New Interpreter's Bible*, Volume VIII, 178.

Instead, I trust that God remains present as our support when troubles overwhelm us. Prayer brings me relief not by solving my problems but by providing strength to keep going.

While the psalmist's promise that God will always provide what we need may not align with our reality, these words describe exactly how we feel when we ache for rescue from our suffering:

O taste and see that the LORD is good;
    happy are those who take refuge in him.
O fear the LORD, you his holy ones;
    for those who fear him have no want.
The young lions suffer want and hunger,
    but those who seek the LORD lack no good thing.

Come, O children, listen to me;
    I will teach you the fear of the LORD.

Many are the afflictions of the righteous,
    but the LORD rescues them from them all.
He keeps all their bones;
    not one of them will be broken.
Evil brings death to the wicked,
    and those who hate the righteous will be condemned.
The LORD redeems the life of his servants;
    none of those who take refuge in him will be
    condemned.—Psalm 34:8-11, 19-22

Taking refuge in God is a blessing. The psalmist writes with absolute certainty that God will care for us, protect us, and provide for us. I see this as a poet describing hope for God's refuge. I don't believe the details match our lived reality, but since when are the details of poetry meant to be literal? The point is that when we lack material things, when we are in trouble, even when our bones are broken, God continues to be present with us. God is our strength to get through these things. I *like* the idea that God will condemn the wicked, but these words aren't spoken to the wicked; they are offered as reassurance to those who are hurt.

Through spiritual poverty, I recognize God not as a problem-solver but as a presence within my struggles. God offers us a place to go, a place to hide and rest and recover, in the middle of both physical and psychological storms. God does not stop the raging outside, but provides quiet, guidance, and comfort. When I pretend that I have the power to fight the storm, I am not living a life of spiritual poverty. This is the trap I fall into: if God is not controlling the world, I seem to think *I* should control it. Spiritual poverty means acknowledging that I am not in control, admitting I don't know the future, and living in the moment without despair, grasping, or desperate attempts to bring about the outcomes I want.

The idea that God orchestrates everything and has a plan for everyone often deteriorates into the toxic theology that good things happen because I am good and bad things happen because I am not. Many people lacking material resources internalize this message, whether they know it or not, and begin to believe that they *deserve* less. Indeed, our culture reinforces this lie, insisting that if those who are poor lived more faithfully or wisely, then they would prosper. This is the Puritan work ethic, our nation's unfortunate founding theology, which views material success as a sign of God's favor.

## Humility

Spiritual poverty requires humility before both God and our neighbors. Psalm 25 talks about the "fear of the LORD"—a concept better understood as awe, reverence, humility, and a recognized dependance on God. Drawing close to God means following God's way rather than our own.

> To you, O LORD, I lift up my soul.
> O my God, in you I trust;
> do not let me be put to shame;

do not let my enemies exult over me.
Do not let those who wait for you be put to shame;
let them be ashamed who are wantonly treacherous.

Make me to know your ways, O LORD;
teach me your paths.
Lead me in your truth and teach me,
for you are the God of my salvation;
for you I wait all day long.

Be mindful of your mercy, O LORD, and of your steadfast love,
for they have been from of old.
Do not remember the sins of my youth or my transgressions;
according to your steadfast love remember me,
for the sake of your goodness, O LORD!

Good and upright is the LORD;
therefore he instructs sinners in the way.
He leads the humble in what is right
and teaches the humble his way.
All the paths of the LORD are steadfast love and faithfulness,
for those who keep his covenant and his decrees.

For your name's sake, O LORD,
pardon my guilt, for it is great.
Who are they who fear the LORD?
He will teach them the way that they should choose.

They will abide in prosperity,
and their children shall possess the land.
The friendship of the LORD is for those who fear him,
and he makes his covenant known to them.

My eyes are ever toward the LORD,
for he will pluck my feet out of the net.

Turn to me and be gracious to me,
for I am lonely and afflicted.
Relieve the troubles of my heart,
and bring me out of my distress.
Consider my affliction and my trouble,
and forgive all my sins.

Consider how many are my foes
and with what violent hatred they hate me.
O guard my life and deliver me;
do not let me be put to shame, for I take refuge in you.
May integrity and uprightness preserve me,
for I wait for you.

Redeem Israel, O God,
out of all its troubles.—Psalm 25

This psalm connects poverty of spirit with experiencing an appropriate amount of shame—essentially feeling embarrassed when we do wrong (verse 3). It was common in biblical times to accept that shame is what keeps us on the right path. Today, our psychological understanding has shifted somewhat, distinguishing between an unhealthy, toxic shame about who we are and the more healthy guilt that is tied to what we've done. I feel guilty when I make a mistake, but I do not feel shame as if I *am* a mistake. The poor in spirit recognize their own wrongdoing and are humble enough to correct unethical or unjust behaviors.

This psalm teaches us that closeness to God requires accepting God's guidance rather than finding our own way. This does not mean that there is preset plan for our lives, but rather that we prioritize God's values. The work of discernment—consulting with others, with the Bible, and with the tradition of theological thought—exemplifies spiritual poverty. It is humbling to look at these rich sources of truth and humility as a reminder that we don't have all the answers ourselves.

Humility is also a matter of dependence. It includes the realization that the things we possess in the material world are not really *ours*. Instead, everything belongs to God. As God's people and agents in the world, we, as a collective, oversee creation. The ideas that individuals can claim natural resources, that a business possesses land, or that we personally own homes, food, and clothing contradict core Christian concepts. The land belongs to God; we merely care for and work our share of it. Early Christians held their possessions in common. The disciples shared one purse. We may manage the resources of the world, but they remain God's.

The practical application of this should be obvious: those with few material resources have a right to a larger share of God's creation. When people apply for food stamps, welfare, or Medicaid, they aren't asking for something that belongs to someone else. They're claiming what should belong to them. They are asking to be given their share of what God provides for us all. Psalm 25:13 promises prosperity for those who fear the LORD. Relatedly, those of us with excess must recognize that withholding these resources means hanging on to something that is not ours. We are being called to help ensure the prosperity of our neighbors.

When I was in junior high, our youth group held a "starvathon" to raise money for the Heifer Project. We fasted for twenty-four hours, spending the night at the church, playing games. The next afternoon, adult volunteers served us dinner to break our fast. However, this dinner did not go as we, the students, expected. For one lucky third of our group, they brought out plates piled with rice, vegetables, and a quarter of a chicken. For another third, they handed out a simple bowl of rice, and then, for the remainder, only a glass of water. The adults serving us explained that this is roughly the breakdown of food inequality in our world.

I laughed—I was so hungry and thrilled that I got the full dinner! My sister, however, did not get the full dinner and did not see the humor in it. In the end, as good Christian teenagers, we immediately began sharing our meals. I pulled off a chicken leg and handed it to my sister, while splitting my veggies with another. Others around us did the same. At the time, I felt quite generous and pleased with my willingness to share.

But was that really generosity? Was that food even mine? What besides random chance gave me authority to decide whether my sister received a leg or a breast or nothing at all? How did I gain the role of the giver and not receiver? True humility would recognize that all the food belonged to all of us. We could have pooled everything and redistributed it equally rather than hoping and relying on the charity of each individual to share some from their plate with others who had none.

## Accepting Help

But I didn't want help redistributing my dinner. Even now, I don't want help passing on my excess to others. Spiritual poverty demands we develop the humility to recognize we do need help and then accept the help we need. People living in poverty often decline help because they want to avoid being a "burden" to others. Meanwhile, those with wealth often insist that they don't need anything.

Society assumes that those who are poor demand government benefits, yet the reality is that many who qualify never apply. Fewer than half of eligible elderly adults apply for SNAP benefits, and only a quarter of those who qualify for Temporary Assistance for Needy

Families (TANF) try to enroll.[17] Every church I've served has members who need food from our food pantry but refuse to use it.

Similarly, those who see themselves as givers often cannot imagine receiving from others. Many who attend the mission workshops I offer cannot identify a single need of their own. This is not because they lack needs, but because they struggle with the humility and sense of interdependence that makes it okay to need help. It is difficult in our society to trust that needs are not weaknesses. I think about the lunches we provide at our street church, where some volunteers are uncomfortable sitting and eating the food they brought. We all need to eat! It's lunchtime! We find ourselves living in an era of loneliness and disconnection, all the while insisting that we don't need help.

American culture prizes independence above all. From the time we are two or three years old, we learn to say "I can do it myself" and are encouraged to maintain that attitude as we grow and mature. While independence is a core American value, it is not a Christian one. The Christian story focuses on interdependence—working together to meet one another's needs. Our identity as neighbors and siblings in faith communicates these essential interconnections.

Accepting our interdependence and our need for help requires humility, and receiving gifts from others builds our spiritual poverty. But humility does not mean humiliation. God intends for all of us to have what we need. When people choose to serve as God's hands and feet, when our government chooses to provide for everyone out of our abundant wealth, then accepting this support means acknowledging that God is providing for us and for our household. This is not charity; this is not pity; this is our rightful share of the whole.

Resisting help from others separates us from God. We know that God is present with us, but we must also recognize that God appears to us as people offering assistance when we need it. And we

---

17. Desmond, *Poverty By America*, 89.

need to learn to say yes. Spiritual poverty is recognizing this and saying yes to help. I have to admit that I do not have it all. So do you. As you pray and reflect this Lent, look for something that you need. As you reflect, be humble in your presumptions of what you know and what you still need to discover. This is the path that leads you to God. Knowing your needs allows you to acknowledge your dependence upon God.

## Solidarity

We also need to learn about the real needs of those who are materially poor. Rather than guessing or assuming, spiritual poverty calls us to be in solidarity with those who do not have enough. Solidarity requires knowing and listening to people. It means making sure that the people who live in material poverty are leading the work of charity and the work to change systems. Charity is the term we use for providing necessary material goods while changing systems eliminates the root causes of poverty. Doing either of these requires a strong relationship with people who are poor. It requires solidarity, and solidarity requires humility.

Solidarity *can* include giving up our own excess and living more simply for the benefit of those who are poor. However, voluntary poverty can also downplay the destructive nature of material poverty. It implies that people might "better themselves" by choosing poverty. It is good to use more of our excess to fight against poverty, but we must avoid any idea that material poverty is a good or beneficial thing.

The United States maintains significant economic segregation between those who are poor and those who are wealthy. Most of the people we work with, exercise with, talk with, or live near have an economic profile that is similar to our own. It is rare to find ourselves making social connections with people of a different economic status by mere chance. Building relationships across economic divides takes effort.

Consider joining a club or a team with an economically diverse make-up. Volunteer for programs that allow you to meet and have genuine conversations with participants who have different economic circumstances. Connect with lower-wage workers in your workplace. One of my parishioners found a walking partner by befriending the people who worked the meat and bakery counters at the local grocery store. This parishioner didn't just learn their names, but asked about their day and their family and, in the process, learned about their passions and vision for the world. Building these relationships will take time, but solidarity begins with these simple connections.

## Conclusion

Spiritual poverty is available to those who have plenty and those that have little, although it may be easier for those with less to access it. We are all dependent on God, but it requires humility to see that we do not have control of the universe. And yet, whether we trust it or not, God is present with us, eager for a relationship. Everything belongs to God, who is present with us. The work of spiritual poverty is recognizing how we are interdependent with all of God's children. This means we must accept help *from* others and give help *to* others.

This giving and receiving is done through acts of charity and by working to change systems. We will address both of these in the chapters that follow.

## LENTEN REFLECTIONS

### A DAILY PRAYER FOR THE FOURTH WEEK OF LENT

Holy one, help us to see you as present with us, as available to us. Guide us in our struggle for humility; help us to get closer to you. Forgive us the ways we try to run the world without you. Holy one, help us to see you in all whom we meet. Amen.

### FOURTH WEEK OF LENT

#### MONDAY REFLECTIONS • Humility

What are the ways you practice humility? What are you humble about? Where does pride appear in your life? Are pride and humility opposites in your mind? Can they coexist? How can you find true pride while still remaining humble? Are there some topics about which you strive to know all the answers? How has the desire to be right shaped the story of your life? How has humility shaped your life? What childhood messages did you hear about humility? How are they still influencing you?

#### TUESDAY REFLECTIONS • Dependence

What areas of your life require you to be dependent on others? In what ways were you dependent on others growing up? How has that shaped your understanding of dependence as an adult? How does relying on others prepare you to rely on God? How is dependence on others different from dependence on God? When have needed to seek God out as a refuge? What happened then? How has that story shaped your understanding of dependence? Is that a story you can return to when trying to depend on God?

## WEDNESDAY REFLECTIONS • Solidarity

When have you truly felt solidarity with another group of people? What did it look like? How did it come about? How did that solidarity make you feel? Did you see the effects of this solidarity in others in the group? Are you a part of groups that you wish you knew better? What might you do to create a sense of solidarity? Are there groups that you would like to become a part of? What are the first steps to getting to know these people and creating a sense of solidarity with them?

## THURSDAY REFLECTIONS • Doing More

What struggles do you have with spiritual poverty? Are there moments in your life where you wish you could have exhibited more spiritual poverty? What more could you have done to achieve that spiritual poverty? What can you do now to work on becoming spiritually poor? What is keeping you from doing those things? What mental and emotional hang ups do you have about spiritual poverty?

## FRIDAY REFLECTIONS • Relationships

Who in your life has a financial situation that is different from your own? How significant are these differences? How much do you know about their finances and how this affects their life? What connections can you develop with this person and others who are in similar situations? What are some ways you can start to make new relationships with people who are different from you? Where would you find people like this?

## SATURDAY REFLECTIONS • Accepting Help

How clearly can you identify your own needs? Do you feel pride when you think that you don't need help? Is that good or bad? Why do you think that? How do you encourage yourself to accept help?

Are you someone who is able to ask for help? Are there situations where you could ask for help more often? What actions can you take to encourage yourself to do this? Is there something you need that makes you feel too afraid or too vulnerable to ask others to help with? What makes it feel this way?

## SUNDAY REFLECTIONS • Celebrating Our Connection to God

Think about a time when you felt especially close to God. What was special about this moment? How did it make you feel? What was happening in your life? Did you seek out this closeness with God? If so, what did you do? How did this closeness affect you? Do you feel like humility and a sense of dependence played a role in getting closer to God? How might they play a role in getting closer to God again?

# INTERLUDE

## A Ministry of Presence

I arrived early to my knitting group in Waltham. The tiny kitchen filled with the smell of various dinners as some women cooked, others ate, and a few were cleaning up after finishing their meals. Two women chatted with each other, while others focused on their food, books, or phones.

As I settled in, I visited for a bit with Victoria, a resident who wanted to talk before our knitting group began. Together, our group rearranged the crowded living room filled with enough couches and stuffed chairs to accommodate the fifteen women who stay at this shelter. I brought donated supplies with me: yarn, knitting needles, crotchet hooks, and patterns for sweaters, shawls, hats, and scarves. As we prepared, I placed a few items on each of the three coffee tables in the middle of the room and sat down with my own knitting.

In the chair beside me sat the green yarn reserved for Juanita; she was making a sweater and had waited weeks for a donation of matching skeins. Anita joined us after washing her dishes, and gradually other women drifted into the room. Five to seven residents typically gather on Tuesday evenings—some to knit, others simply to join in the conversation. When I invited a woman lingering in the doorway to sit with us, she quietly declined.

Then, we knit.

Conversation flowed back and forth about assorted frustrations like missed appointments and endless waits for housing. Weariness is a constant theme, whether from making the long trek between places that offer services or coming home after a long day at work. The women exchanged advice with one another, shared job leads, and offered encouragement. But mostly, we just talked like people do: How's the weather? What's in the news? How did the Red Sox or the Patriots do last weekend? Someone mentioned an annoying boyfriend; another complained about a late train or bus, and everyone agreed that lettuce prices have become absurd.

Wanda serves as our knitting expert. Despite bringing my own project, I'm not really qualified to offer much help myself. Wanda moved from seat to seat, rescuing dropped stitches and clarifying confusing patterns. Some women finished only a couple of rows during our two hours together; others got halfway through a hat.

Keeping regular volunteers for this program can be challenging. They grow frustrated with what seems like a lack of purpose or direction. As we leave each week, some volunteer always suggests how I should have advised one woman to find a job or warned another about not spending so much money on take out. But these volunteers misunderstand our ministry. This ministry is about sitting and talking. It's a ministry about being present.

Of course, there's more to it than that. Presence helps create a sense of normalcy in these women's disrupted lives. We offer space to unwind and just be. Social workers provide necessary guidance and tell people what they should do next, and I am grateful for their work with these women. But our ministry is knitting, nothing more. We don't make anything to sell. We don't pressure people to share their life stories. Through patient presence, we build trust. Sometimes, a woman calls asking for help. Sometimes I talk about the struggles and need in my own life. But mostly, we just knit.

# 5

# Charity

## My Story

In junior high, I was so excited to be confirmed because it granted me voting rights at church meetings. At my first such meeting, the congregation debated whether we should repaint the sanctuary and whether we should paint it blue or white. I won't lie; I was a little underwhelmed. I leaned over to my dad and whispered, "Shouldn't we spend this money on mission instead?"

"We need the building to do mission," he replied.

I voted yes—and blue—along with the majority of those present.

My family took charity seriously. Where others displayed cross-stitched messages like "God Bless This Home" on their walls, my parents have "Faith Without Works Is Dead" hanging on theirs. In our household, faith and charity were inseparable. Church provided a place for worship and learning, but these both served to guide our purpose and engage in mission. Working with the Fresh Air Fund, our family hosted kids from New York City at our suburban home for the summer.[18] We picked up trash on the side of the road and planted flowers for Earth Day. We raised money for all sorts of

18. When my family took part in the Fresh Air Fund, the organization sent youth from New York City to live with suburban and rural families for several weeks each summer. The Fund now sends the youth to rural summer camps.

things through bike-a-thons, walk-a-thons, and dance-a-thons. To me, this was simply what Christians did.

Shortly after the Vietnam War ended, my mother decided that our congregation should sponsor refugees. The economy was pretty bad at the time, particularly for our working-class church members, and there was a lot of arguing about whether we could handle this type of work.

I remember the story my mother told upon returning home after the decisive meeting. One particularly cantankerous member turned to my mom at the last moment and asked, "Why should we do this?"

"I think it is what Jesus says to do," she replied.

He sat back, sighed deeply, and said, "Well, if you have that much faith, we have to go with it."

And we did.

Years later, when I lived on my own, I volunteered at Rainbow Place, Rockville Presbyterian Church's homeless shelter. Once I started seminary, I began thinking about how my role as a pastor could focus on helping and serving those who are poor.

The questions that had seemed simple to answer when I was child seemed much harder now. I had seen churches sponsor refugees to mixed results. Our fundraising often felt insignificant relative to the need. Churches traditionally spend little of their budget on mission work, and our efforts yield only modest results. Reality rarely seems to live up to our ideal. Nevertheless I still believe that Christians are called to do acts charity, despite the somewhat frustrating outcomes.

Scripture demands charity and generosity. Jesus gives us example after example of this including the widow that gives up all she has. This directive to give and give generously is not limited to those with plenty. All of us, poor and wealthy alike, are asked to give out of what we have. If you have anything, give. If you have excess, give more. If we want to know Jesus, then we must recall that the story of the sheep and the goats insists that Jesus *is* the poor. During this

Lenten season, I encourage you to spend some time reflecting on how to be in relationship with those in poverty and how you learn to help address their material needs.

## The Apartment

Alyssa and her friend Rosa sat together looking for apartments to rent, but found few viable options.

"I can't find any apartments for $1,200, or even $1,500," Alyssa said.

"I think you need a room to rent instead," Rosa suggested.

Alyssa sighed in frustration. "Where I can bring my cat?" She entered another search. "Here is one for $1,800."

"An apartment?" Rosa asked hopefully.

"No. A room in a house—no pets allowed."

Alyssa earns $2,000 a month and recently got divorced. During her marriage, she and her ex-husband qualified for the state's affordable housing program, and their mortgage was only $1,200 per month. Now, however, she owes him half the home's value. With little equity and having her job for a short time, she can't take over the mortgage alone.

Market-rate apartments in her area run around $2,000 per month—her entire income. Her poverty has forced her into a situation where she must abandon an affordable mortgage for an impossible rent. Only Rosa's charity—offering to cover first month, last month, and the security deposit—makes it possible to rent a single room.

Alyssa could have made different choices. She could have stayed in a bad marriage; she could have held out hope to find a higher paying job, or she could have relocated to a new city entirely. But her support system is here, her job, while not high-paying, allows her to work from home, saving the costs of a car. And do we really want to say that poverty means someone should be forced to stick out a marriage that isn't healthy?

But this is reality for the working poor. These are the choices they face.

## Charitable Giving Is Good for You

It's good to give in general, and it's even better to give to those in need. I mean that literally; it actually *feels* good. Those who give feel like they are making a difference. They are using what they have for good. This gives a boost to self-esteem and allows people to think they're a good person. This is true from a physiological perspective too. When we give, we get a dopamine hit. Charitable giving can snap us out of restlessness or a sustained funk. It can even relieve the symptoms of mild depression.

We have a tendency to downplay the good feelings that accompany giving, and that makes sense too. It feels self-centered to make giving about what you, as the giver, get in return. It's true that giving should be focused on what the receiver needs, but it's also okay to feel good about doing a good thing. It is a beneficial to feel positively about being concerned for the common good and following the path God has set out for you.

## Consider Jesus' words in Luke 12:

> Sell your possessions and give alms. Make purses for yourselves that do not wear out, an unfailing treasure in heaven, where no thief comes near and no moth destroys. For where your treasure is, there your heart will be also.—Luke 12:33-34

To align your heart with God, sell what you have. Note that the benefit in this passage comes to the person with possessions—by giving alms, they find themselves closer to God. While alms are assumed to be something good for others, that's not the primary point Jesus is making.

It's interesting that Jesus does not instruct us to give our *belongings* to the poor. Instead, we are told to sell them and give alms from the cash received. This implies that we are meant to give away all of the proceeds of the sale. The purse in question is not a place to put what we've earned from selling our possessions, but a metaphorical place to put the treasure we have received from God.

In Acts, the blessing is again offered to the giver rather than claiming that the giving conveys a blessing to the recipient:

> "In all this I have given you an example that by such work we must support the weak, remembering the words of the Lord Jesus, for he himself said, 'It is more blessed to give than to receive.'"—Acts 20:35

Look at these passages again. We are told to give, commanded to give, but there are no conditions placed on those who receive. We often craft unwritten rules for those to whom we give: they must show gratitude; they must be careful with what we give them. Certainly, alms should never be used for vices like alcohol, drugs, lottery tickets, or cigarettes, nor for junk food or sugary drinks. Those who receive should also refrain from buying luxury items like a big TV or fancy steaks. But these rules for those who receive are not based in the scriptures. The point of the giving, according to these passages, is to help the giver connect with God, to get closer to God. It does not matter what the receiver does with the gift once it's been given.

Let's think for a moment about Matthew 25:31-46, the story of the sheep and the goats and one of our most commonly referenced scriptures about charity. This passage says nothing about how those who need food, drink, clothing, welcome, healing, or someone to visit them in prison will be judged. It is those who have given that are blessed and those who have not that are damned. This text suggests that final judgment will be based solely on our care for the hungry, the thirsty, those without clothes, those who are ill, those who are strangers, and those in prison. Note that Jesus does not say that we are being like God when we give, but rather that we are giving *to* God.

## A Story

When I arrived at Savers, a local for-profit thrift store, to dispose of many things I no longer needed, I quickly realized that I was not alone in my need to purge. Apparently, many others also needed to get rid of their excess that day, and the parking lot was crowded with people lugging boxes, bags, and furniture out of their vehicles. A huge bureau and several bicycles were set on the sidewalk; toys overflowed a massive bin, and there were racks and racks and piles and piles of used clothing.

Where does all this stuff come from? Well, on that day, a large pile of it came from my car. We've come a long way from the days when we packed all our most prized possessions into a covered wagon and headed west. Out of all the stuff we have, what is it that we really need?

Some of us were raised with a Depression-era mentality. Our parents taught us to save everything. Much of what we keep exists only for potential emergencies. Others are beautiful or have sentimental value. Personally, I have several teapots covered in dust sitting in my kitchen—each one a memory of friends, trips, or churches I have served.

But do those who are poor need my tea pots? Do they need my old games and used clothing? I'm skeptical, yet I still find myself at Savers or the Salvation Army or Goodwill, thinking I have fulfilled my obligation to meet the needs of others today.

As I left Savers that day, a father opened the car door and helped his young son from the car. The boy was maybe three or four years old. Once his son was situated safely on the ground, the dad handed him the biggest toy fire truck I have ever seen. It was a mountain of shiny red plastic topped with a blue seat, and the boy had to extend his arms as far as he could to carry this toy into the donation center. The look on his face was neither happy nor sad—simply determined. His dad walked close behind, saying nothing as they navigated through the crowded parking lot.

I wondered what I was witnessing. What was the goal for their mission today? Was the little boy learning that to get new stuff, you must first give your old stuff away? Was he doing penance for misbehavior? Had had he come home from daycare one day upset about some small injustice in the world—another kid like him who didn't have any toys perhaps? Had his parents gently guided him to find a way to give something to those in need? Was he the one making the decision to give away his fire truck?

I have no idea. And I never will. I hope it was something deep and meaningful, but I don't know what's ultimately right. It's not *wrong* to give our stuff away, but I worry that this model gives us permission to accumulate more and more. Does it allow us to get off easy and soothe our guilt when we give away our unwanted possessions to others? Should others have the responsibility to soothe our guilt?

## Giving to Relieve My Excess

The truth is that much of our giving is not really about people who are poor. Most of us haven't checked to understand what people living in poverty need, nor have we checked to make sure that what we're offering will help. Some of what we're giving—maybe even a lot of what we're giving—is offered because we have to do something about the stuff overflowing our homes. Overbuying and hoarding create a common storage challenge for middle and high-income people. We have too much—clothing especially, but also furniture and household items—and when we are confronted by this fact, we decide to declutter. It's too painful to see the items we bought placed in the trash, so we look for places to donate them. It's not that we *don't* care about people who are poor, it's just that the caring isn't motivating the giving.

It's fascinating to think about how much we care about where our excess goes. First, we prefer giving to people we know. Community clothing swaps thrive on the principle that you can get rid of your stuff and take back a little of what others have donated. What's leftover is then donated somewhere else. Hopefully, it's donated to the *right* place. I've not yet figured out what makes a place the *right* place or why it matters that the things I'm getting rid of need to go there, but it's definitely something I look for. I just think that some of my things are nicer, you know? They deserve to go somewhere suitable—it's my waste, but not my trash, right?

I think you can see the pattern here. The primary concern is not what's best for people who need material resources, but what is best for me—for my standards, for my state of mind. We know what the most useful gift is for people in need: cash. But we have a deeply held bias against that. We want restraints on how the money is used, but this keeps us from helping people in the best way that we can, the way that allows them to respond to their own needs.

## Charity in Jesus' Time

In the first century, giving charity to the poorest of the poor meant giving to beggars and providing work to the working poor. From the beginning, the church welcomed and cared for the poor, not by giving to individuals directly but by sharing meals. Early Christians helped anyone who asked, and they shared what they had. Several non-Christian writers from the time poke fun at Christian communities because of this behavior. Lucian of Samosata (c. 125–180) notes how easy it is to take advantage of Christians:

> "[T]heir first lawgiver persuaded them that they are all brothers of one another after they have transgressed once, for all by denying the Greek gods and by worshipping that crucified sophist himself and living under his laws. Therefore they despise all things indiscriminately and consider them common property, receiving such doctrines traditionally without any definite evidence. So if any charlatan and trickster, able to profit by occasions, comes among them, he quickly acquires sudden wealth by imposing upon simple folk."[19]

The culture of that time, much like the culture of our time, placed more importance on not being tricked by the dishonest than caring for the people who really needed it.

In the fourth century, the place of Christians in culture shifted. In *Unjust Steward: Wealth, Poverty, and the Church Today,* Miguel Escobar describes how the Emperor Constantine negotiated with bishops to create an institutional church that aligned itself with the empire. The agreement exempted the church from persecution and taxation and, in exchange, the church assumed responsibility for caring for all the empire's poor.[20] The church, along with its distinctive work of caring for the poor, became subsumed within the dominant culture rather than standing in contrast to it. Did we give up the heart of our faith? Did care for the poor become an obligation rather than a calling? I'm afraid we lost out in that bargain.

---

19. Lucian of Samosata, "The Passing of Peregrinus," A. M. Harmon, trans., in *Loeb Classical Library,* 9 volumes (Harvard University Press). extracted for the web by Roger Pearse, 2001. Paragraph #13, https://www.tertullian.org/rpearse/lucian/peregrinus.htm. Accessed March 28, 2025.
20. Miguel Escobar, *The Unjust Steward: Wealth, Poverty, and the Church Today* (Cincinnati, OH: Forward Movement, 2022), 271.

## Charity vs. Sharing

Charitable organizations collect material goods from those with excess and distribute them to those in need. Donors give out of their surplus or buy what is needed, then the organization passes it along. It's a tidy little system.

Early Christian communities practiced something different: they simply ate together. The people who could afford food or who grew food brought food and sat together with those who brought nothing. They embodied the idea of spiritual poverty, trusting that God would provide through the community. When everyone is sharing dinner with one another every night, the kingdom of God becomes plainly visible. It's right here! That sense of community and sharing must have been just as important as the food.

*Sharing,* unlike charity, emerges from solidarity with those who are poor. We share with people we know. I once visited a church in Brighton, Massachusetts. This church didn't just have a meal program, but an entire church supper that was open to and attended by people throughout the community. Church members and community members volunteered together, cooked together, and then ate together.

This is the way Jesus showed us. Jesus and his disciples lived as a community. They traveled together and shared a common purse. The early church described in Acts 2 continued this practice, sustained by patrons who provided funds for the gathered community:

> All who believed were together and had all things in common; they would sell their possessions and goods and distribute the proceeds to all, as any had need. Day by day, as they spent much time together in the temple, they broke bread at home and ate their food with glad and generous hearts, praising God and having the goodwill of all the people. And day by day the Lord added to their number those who were being saved.—Acts 2:44-47

While this lifestyle sounds unbelievable by modern American standards, Reta Halteman Finger's book *Of Widows and Meals* reveals that it was common for first-century subsistence workers to share resources among family and friends. The radical element here is the creation of a fictional family that crosses class boundaries. As Finger writes, "An ordinary meal eaten with people of different social positions is in reality *not* an ordinary meal."[21] The tie binding together this community is not blood, but the Holy Spirit. In response to the Spirit, the people recognized that what they own belongs to God and is meant to be shared equitably by God's people. They became each other's family, gathering at the temple and in homes:

> Now the whole group of those who believed were of one heart and soul, and no one claimed private ownership of any possessions, but everything they owned was held in common. With great power the apostles gave their testimony to the resurrection of the Lord Jesus, and great grace was upon them all. There was not a needy person among them, for as many as owned lands or houses sold them and brought the proceeds of what was sold.—Acts 4:32-35

The church potluck remains our closest approximation of this first-century practice. Can we imagine expanding this model to address the material needs of our much broader, wider spiritual family, the body of Christ? To truly replicate the early church, we would need to find a way to include a vast array of people crossing all social boundaries. As Paul declares in Galatians 3:28, our spiritual family should transcend divisions of race, class, and gender.

---

21. Reta Halteman Finger, *Of Widows and Meals: Communal Meals in the Book of Acts* (Grand Rapids, MI: William B. Eerdmans Publishing Company, 2007), 277 and 230, italics original.

## Beyond the Potluck

Whenever you find yourself reading this, you can be assured that there will be moments of economic turbulence. Food prices will rise; unemployment will become an issue, and government safety nets will get smaller or develop new cracks for people to slip through. New laws and regulations will have unexpected and unwanted side-effects. It's true today as I write this, and it will be true again in the future. Whenever you are reading this, there are people who need help.

We already have people in our churches who need material help to meet their basic needs. Isn't that what we do best—care for one another? What would it take to share more and share better, both with other church members and with our neighbors?

Giving people cash to spend as they choose provides the most effective support. It feels countercultural just to say that out loud! Is it really that simple? Can we just *give* people money? But think about this, why can't we just hand out $50 bills? Why can't we set up a fund where those with excess give into it, and then the funds are distributed directly once a month to those who don't have enough? What would happen if we decided to simply make sure that everyone in our parish had enough money to be stable? It's a simple thing, but it's also a big thing.

Consider this scenario: what if every member of your community who makes six figures contributed five or ten thousand dollars annually to a central fund. Then, that fund would be divided equally among all the households that make less than $30,000 a year. Move those numbers around to make them work for your community and your context, but take a moment to dream about what a difference this would make for the people in your congregation who are living in poverty. Consider too how profound giving like this can make a large impact on the life of the giver.

But how do we make sure this is fair? Should we ask for proof of income? Will we require tax forms? The awkwardness alone causes us to hesitate! Perhaps we are afraid that there will be an influx of people who are poor wanting to join our church solely for financial benefit. That fear definitely gives me pause. On the other hand, don't we want more people to join—more people to help, to pledge, and to hear the good news? (Though perhaps I've reversed the proper order of importance.) Are we truly afraid of attracting *too many* new members?

The truth is that it requires less of us emotionally to anonymously support "everyone" through the form of taxes or donations to big nationwide institutions than it does to directly care for other members of our congregation. There's a certain out-of-sight, out-of-mind element to it. However, when we're sharing with our neighbors, when we're making sure that everyone around us has enough, it's plainly visible who needs more. It challenges us to ask ourselves how much we should be sharing. There is the benefit that anonymous giving can redistribute more money more equitably, but that should not keep us from the relationship building that comes with care for our immediate neighbors.

## When Giving Is Hard

Think back to the story of Alyssa from earlier in this chapter. It was easy to empathize with her, to feel her pain, and to want the best for her. You want to help her. But what if that story had slightly different details?

What about someone like Alex, who owns his home but allowed it to fall into disrepair and doesn't make an effort to fix it up? Or Roberto, who sold his house but putters around aimlessly when it's time to pack, and now the buyer needs a court-ordered eviction to get him to move? There's also Juanita, who quit her job and moved in with a neighbor when she realized she was going to lose her home anyway. Lisa demanded a divorce in a rage, and that was the last straw for her husband—her violent outbursts hurt both him and their child. Finally, there's someone like Debbie, who insisted on divorce when her spouse got sober and would no longer binge drink with her.

These stories are messy because people are messy. Are we just as ready to help them?

It's hard to know what's behind the self-destructive behavior of other people. Maybe they get more support if they tell a story about being a victim. Perhaps they have a hidden disability. Maybe they're depressed or angry. Maybe they're just not very nice. The fact is some people who need material resources cheat or fudge things a little in order to get more. SNAP benefits are sold for cash. People lease out rooms in their subsidized housing. And all sorts of people avoid getting married to keep their benefits—people on disability want to avoid a reduction in benefits; people on TANF and other government aid don't want to reduce their income, and older people getting social security based off a divorced or deceased spouse avoid marriage too.

There's nothing original about any of this. People with excess cheat too in all sorts of ways to pay less in taxes.

Some of these rules are bad, but even with perfect rules that cover every exception, we would still find some people cheating to receive benefits. While the number of cheaters is low, it makes some leery to provide resources without restrictions. But then there's the reality behind it all. People make bad decisions; they experience trauma, depression, and a lack of good options. And yes, sometimes they cheat or lie or steal. We can, if we so choose, spend our time wondering if each individual person deserves our help, but is there such a thing as the unworthy poor? I suggest that for Christians, this is not a valid question.

The more important question is whether we would rather have a system that accidentally pays cheaters or a system that accidentally misses out on providing for someone in need. Assuming that the system can't be perfect—and it can't—in which direction is it better to err? The more tests we put in place to avoid cheating, the more people who qualify either decide against applying or are erroneously disqualified. The simpler we can make the application process, the more likely people who need the benefit will receive it.

As Christians, what do we think the proper penalty should be if someone is found to be cheating? What should the penalty be for acting in chronically unwise ways? The penalty for lacking strong executive function? For being a dreamer instead of practical? These are all reasons that people find themselves living in poverty that are ostensibly within their control. Are there worthy and unworthy people in God's eyes? Should these personal failures be the reason a person goes hungry? Goes without housing? Should these failures be the reason they don't have access to healthcare or mental health services? Are those the appropriate punishments?

It's hard to see how Christians can divide people into those who are worthy and unworthy of life's basic necessities, especially when that distinction is based on the bad things they have either done or thought. Forgiveness is an essential part of our faith story. I don't think there is anyone who is unforgivable. Jesus forgave the Roman Empire for his crucifixion without waiting for their contrition. I think we can stand to forgive a whole lot more than we do.

Theologically, we don't have a way to separate the worthy recipients of charity from the unworthy. For those of us who believe in the doctrine of original sin, we know that we are all unworthy. For Christians more focused on God's original blessing, that blessing is on all of us—both those who have done many things wrong and those who have done most things right. None of us have behaved perfectly. Christ is our new Adam, our model for how to be like the first perfectly created being; none of us live up to that model.

## What to Do with Your Excess?

As we strive to follow the model Christ provides, we must ask: What does our faith require us to do with surplus wealth? The simplest answer—and the one Jesus gives to the rich young man in Matthew 19—is to give it away. Donate it. All of it. Or at least as much as you can. Jesus instructs us to sell our belongings and give the money to the poor. Unless you personally know people who are poor, this is difficult to do. Frustratingly, I have not yet found an organization that will give my money directly to people who are poor. Instead, I give to organizations that serve poor people. I choose to give to some organizations that provide direct services and some that engage in political action to change the dynamics of our economy to favor people who are poor.

The National Philanthropic trust reports that religious institutions get a higher percentage of charitable dollars (24%) than any other groups. Educational institutions and organizations focused on human services each get fourteen percent of our dollars. Furthermore, the report states that middle-income Americans donate an average of $3,296 annually.[22] For those of you, like me, who give our largest donations to our church, only a small fraction of these donations directly assist people who are poor.

Much of what is donated to education is sent to private universities and high schools. While some of that is allocated for scholarships, most is not. Similarly, groups focused on healthcare, the arts, and the environment, while noble organizations, designate relatively little of their funding to people who are poor.

When considering our giving, we should ask which options will deepen our connection to the God who guides our lives? This Lent, I seek to discern and follow God's path, and I hope you do as well.

---

22. National Philanthropic Trust, "Charitable Giving Statistics," https://www.nptrust.org/philanthropic-resources/charitable-giving-statistics/. Accessed March 30, 2025.

## Conclusion

Charity makes us feel good! And that is good, as long as the person or organization actually needs what we give. Giving to relieve our excess is not actually charity. One thing we can do to reinforce our sense of interdependence is to think about sharing resources more than giving resources. While direct giving can be transactional with a giver and a receiver, sharing builds relationships. Hopefully, we can do that without judging the people who need material resources.

But people generally need more help than it is easy to give them. To create a just world, we need systemic changes to be sure that all of God's abundance is shared effectively.

## LENTEN REFLECTIONS

### A DAILY PRAYER FOR THE FIFTH WEEK OF LENT

Holy one, help us to see you and build relationships when we are giving material things. Guide us to be generous with what others need. Forgive us when we allow our giving to become impersonal. Holy one, help us to see you in all whom we meet. Amen.

### FIFTH WEEK OF LENT

#### MONDAY REFLECTIONS • Giving

Recall a time when you gave some of your possessions away. How did it make you feel? Did it make you feel good? Does feeling good about it trouble you? If so, why? What do you think about the idea that charity is good for the giver? Is it okay if this is the motivation that prompts you to give? Why or why not?

#### TUESDAY REFLECTIONS • Knowing the Need

How can giving focus on addressing the actual needs of people who are poor? How do you know what these needs are? How can you balance addressing these needs with your own motivations for giving? Do you personally know people who need material support? What kind of support do they need?

#### WEDNESDAY REFLECTIONS • Receiving

When has receiving a gift made you uncomfortable? What kind of discomfort did you feel? Did the discomfort stem from how it was given or the identity of the giver? What's the difference between a birthday or a holiday gift and a gift you receive on another day? How do these gifts differ emotionally? What do you genuinely need right now? How would receiving this as a gift affect you?

### THURSDAY REFLECTIONS • Sharing

What is something you regularly share with others? How does sharing with your family or a close friend feel different from sharing with someone outside your family system? Do you share regularly with your church? Why or why not? Do those at your church feel more like family or someone outside of your family? What are the reasons for this feeling? If you want it to change, how do you think you can effect that change?

### FRIDAY REFLECTIONS • Cheating

How do you feel about rules? Do you tend to lean more toward following rules at all times or more toward situational flexibility? How do you feel about people who don't follow the rules? Think about a time when you have broken or bent a rule. How did it feel to do that? What consequences did you experience? What consequences do you think you should have experienced?

### SATURDAY REFLECTIONS • Something More

What is one thing you can do or change to improve the way you give? Could you build a relationship with someone experiencing poverty? Could you volunteer someplace? Can you support a new organization and make a donation there? How does your giving deepen your connection to God?

### SUNDAY REFLECTIONS • Celebrating Your Giving

What charitable practices bring you pride or joy? What prompted you to give in this way? How did these practices become part of your life? What about these practices makes you smile? How could you extend or deepen these practices?

# INTERLUDE

## Moving Ministry

Lent offers congregations an ideal time to evaluate their charitable practices and discern if they should be doing more. As the largest recipient of charitable giving, churches must ask: How much should we be passing on to those living in poverty? What concrete actions could we do to respond to poverty in our communities?

South Acton Congregational Church in Massachusetts developed a moving ministry, now continued by West Concord Union Church. The ministry literally involves moving people from one home to another. This ministry began in 1972 as a fundraiser—volunteers moved a church member who then donated the amount required for typical moving costs to the church.

Initially, moves were arranged through members, their friends, and friends of friends. When the town's social services office began referring clients to them, it evolved into the church's most significant outreach program. Four to six times a year, ten to twelve parishioners gather at an apartment or small house to help someone move into their next home.

The ministry sets practical boundaries—limiting moves to about fifteen miles—and visits with the family ahead of time to determine how big the truck needs to be for their belongings. Usually, the person receiving moving help is required to be completely packed beforehand (though members of the congregation often help out in the weeks ahead of the move).

While most volunteers simply carry boxes for a few hours, there is some expertise required. Several members excel at the real-life Tetris game of fitting furniture and boxes together in the tight confines of the moving truck. Others have mastered techniques for safely lifting heavy furniture. Someone always brings coffee, and there is a tradition of homemade muffins. Remarkably, the group has never broken, cracked, or lost any item.

The volunteers also take special pride in making sure that the person is fully moved into their new home—the bed is assembled and made, the rugs are put down, and the furniture and lamps are all arranged into just the right place. Recipients consistently comment on how included they feel in the church family during the moving process.

# 6

# Justice

## My Story

Growing up, I took part in what I would call "mild" protests. My family participated in what I suspect was the first nationwide Earth Day event, joining a group collecting trash and planting flowers in our community. We raised money for people who were hungry at bike-a-thons and walk-a-thons. We went to help with Hudson River cleanup efforts. As an adult, I marched against the war in Iraq and in favor of LGBTQIA+ rights.

The churches I've served have all taken part in these types of events together too—peace marches, anti-gun violence demonstrations, and fundraisers for homeless shelters and food banks.

In 2018, I joined in the six-week series of protests organized by the Poor People's Campaign. These gatherings addressed everything from wages to military spending to immigrant rights. We held planning meetings on Thursdays and protested on Mondays. The planning group set up the boundaries for each event and trained those who were willing to risk arrest.

One week, our collective action involved occupying the state house to demand justice for people in poverty and give visibility to the Poor People's Campaign. Our goal was to get a story written up in the newspaper.

In accordance with our training, we made the final decision about whether to break the law—by staying at the state house after it officially closed—as a group. If anyone in our group decided against arrest, we would all head home. Each of us kept $50 in cash, a credit card, and our phones and sent any other items home with our fellow protestors. Nevertheless, we had our doubts about whether the risk we were taking would succeed. The local paper said they would not cover the event, and we didn't see any reporters.

After a short discussion, we made the decision to stay. The police kept their distance while we talked, but once we chose to remain, they approached each of us individually with a plea to just leave voluntarily. Their message was one about caring for ourselves rather than the group. They told us that it wouldn't make a difference. We all chose to remain, singing songs together. The officers waited, likely preferring to arrest us after dark in an attempt to minimize publicity. Around 9 p.m., they zip-tied our hands, separated us into smaller groups, and took us to be processed. Throughout the ride to the station and the booking process, the police repeatedly emphasized, kindly, that we were wasting their time.

After paying our $50 administrative fee late on Saturday night, my fellow protestors and I were released. The protest organizers picked us up and helped us get to where we would be staying that night, while informing us we had a court date at 9 a.m. the next morning.

The next morning, exhausted as I drove into court, I received a call from my brother-in-law.

"Good job Liz!" he exclaimed.

"What happened?"

"You are in the paper!"

"What paper? Wait, what?"

He sent me the link, and there I was looking determined in my white Easter stole adorned with pink flowers as I exited the state house with my hands zip-tied. It was on the front page of section B. We had achieved our goal for the day!

Going through the booking process, it all felt like a waste of time. We were certain the paper wasn't present, and we didn't see photographers. We'd been at the protest from 10 a.m. until after dark. We didn't get home until early the next morning.

Yet our efforts bore fruit—a photograph and an article explaining the campaign's mission.

## Care for the Poor

As Christians, we have a variety of ways to address poverty. Engaging with scripture and poverty during Lent, like you're doing now, means we must also ask essential questions about the role we have in alleviating poverty. What role do people who have plenty have? For that matter, what role should the government have in eliminating poverty and caring for those who are poor?

There are so many questions. How should our community be involved in caring for the poor? What is our role as individuals who live as part of a system? What can our church do? Think back to the common purse shared by Jesus and his disciples. This is also a symbol of the common good. What is our role in the common good?

We seek spiritual poverty. In the process, we aspire to find ourselves living in solidarity with those who are poor. Along the way, we will naturally want to provide charity to meet people's immediate needs. Yet, at the same time, we must recognize that charity is not enough. Poor people make the same mistakes as rich people, but those mistakes affect those who are poor more deeply. In addition, many people who don't make those mistakes, who do the right thing and work hard, still do not get ahead. Solidarity helps us see how the system is rigged against people who are poor.

The truth is that we must change the system. We must remove and dismantle the barriers to banking, healthcare, and education, and improve the supports for people with disabilities, immigrants, and families with children. We must strive to make it so that full-time work is sufficient for economic stability, no matter the job. We must redistribute God's wealth more equitably. These projects all require us to work with the broader community.

## Poverty Is Caused by Abuse: Micah's Witness

While we all know that poverty is not a good thing, the Hebrew Bible also makes it clear that it is caused by outside forces. Gustavo Gutiérrez writes that the Hebrew words translated as "poverty" and "poor" in English evoke the idea of people being bent, hurt, and humiliated by the systems around them. Poverty does not just happen; poverty is caused by injustice.[23]

In the Hebrew Bible, both the law and the prophets prioritize both caring for the poor and devotion to God. The law calls for crops to be set aside for the poor and commands the nation to protect the poor. In the prophets, care for the poor is synonymous with faithfulness. The prophet Micah is an example of this, telling the leaders that their ongoing theft and greed will lead to the nation's judgment and destruction. Micah even provides three systemic causes of poverty: hoarding land, dishonest courts, and exploitation in business. In Micah's time, land was the primary means of income, food, and wealth:

> Woe to those who devise wickedness
>     and evil deeds on their beds!
> When the morning dawns, they perform it,
>     because it is in their power.
> They covet fields and seize them,
>     houses and take them away;
> they oppress householder and house,
>     people and their inheritance.
> Therefore thus says the LORD:

23. Gutiérrez, *A Theology of Liberation,* 165.

Now, I am devising against this family an evil
from which you cannot remove your necks,
and you shall not walk arrogantly,
for it will be an evil time.—Micah 2:1-3

Coveting leads to taking land and homes from others, presumably as collection on unpaid debts. But the land, along with the fruits of the land, belong to the people collectively rather than to a single person. The crime is that the people as a whole do not reap the benefits of the land. In Leviticus 25:23, God insists that the land cannot be sold; it belongs to God; we are but the tenants. Our bankruptcy laws provide some level of protection to a person's home, for instance, but we continue to experience the historical problem of overwhelming debt that can wipe out a family's stability for generations:

Hear this, you rulers of the house of Jacob
and chiefs of the house of Israel,
who abhor justice
and pervert all equity,
who build Zion with blood
and Jerusalem with wrong!
Its rulers give judgment for a bribe;
its priests teach for a price;
its prophets give oracles for money;
yet they lean upon the LORD and say,
"Surely the LORD is with us!
No harm shall come upon us."
Therefore because of you
Zion shall be plowed as a field;
Jerusalem shall become a heap of ruins,
and the mountain of the temple a wooded height.
—Micah 3:9-12

The prophet accuses government leaders of accepting bribes for judgments and for being opposed to equity. The leaders, who in that time would simultaneously be both religious and government authorities, believe God will protect them. On the contrary, Micah says this behavior will lead to the destruction of Jerusalem itself, which does come to pass in 722 BCE.

Our own judicial system also struggles to provide equal justice. Bail bonds and court fees punish the poor far more severely than the wealthy; access to legal aid is uneven, and both juries and judges struggle with ingrained biases. Furthermore, our prisons, which are not really designed to focus on rehabilitation, keep families separated by not extending visiting rights to former felons. I met one parent who was wracked with guilt over how his own crime and subsequent prison time now separated him from his son, who is currently in prison for his own crimes. I simply can't see how this system isn't perpetuating the cycle of violence.

> Can I forget the treasures of wickedness in the house of the wicked
> and the despicable false measure?
> Can I tolerate wicked scales
> and a bag of dishonest weights?
> Your wealthy are full of violence;
> your inhabitants speak lies
> with tongues of deceit in their mouths.
> Therefore I have begun to strike you down,
> making you desolate because of your sins.
> —Micah 6:10-13

The prophet Micah declares that poverty is perpetuated by dishonest trade and that God will not tolerate this. Like Jesus' woes to the rich, here God promises desolation. While it might be that individual business leaders are the problem, the punishment here is on the nation, so I believe Micah is speaking of systemic abuse of the poor in the markets. The nation is failing in its role to promote equity through laws and proper enforcement. Our local, state, and federal governments can, and should, strive to reduce the ways that employers, banks, healthcare organizations, and others take advantage of people with few resources. They can (and today, sometimes do) implement programs to protect people from dishonest trade, punish corruption, and limit the ability to seize homes and property. They can develop programs that prioritize low-cost housing, a living wage, and affordable food. All of these are systemic strategies for reducing poverty.

In the Hebrew Bible, God speaks to the leaders of the nation through the prophets. In our own time, to whom is God speaking? This Lent, is God speaking through us as a church and as individuals? Is God asking us to speak to the leaders of our own town, state, and nation? What is God telling us to say?

## How to Help People Who Work

Most people of working age who are experiencing poverty are also employed. Most children who live in poverty live with adults who have jobs. Beyond that, almost all people who are not working either want to be working or have a disability that prevents them from working.[24] Nevertheless, these working people are still poor. We must change the system we live in so that people who are working make enough to have stability. They must be able to earn enough to afford housing, healthcare, and food with enough left over to save for emergencies. Part-time workers need to be treated fairly. They need a way to access benefits, and they need schedules that are regular enough to allow for more than one job if necessary. Full-time workers need a living wage. This would be justice.

24. Ryan Finnigan and Emily Pearly, "Work and Poverty," *The EconoFact Network*, 2023, https://econofact.org/work-and-poverty. Accessed March 21, 2025.

The United States offers a significant tax benefit to the working poor called the Earned Income Tax Credit (EITC). It reduces taxes that a worker pays and can also be a direct grant designed to help those who work get ahead. In 2024, families with two children, filing jointly, with income up to $62,688 could qualify for as much as $6,960.[25] There are a few other qualifications that affect eligibility; for instance, significant investment income reduces the payment, and the payout is much lower for those without children.

This all sounds great, but it can also cause issues. There are some who would argue that the EITC creates problems of its own. On one hand, this tax credit effectively subsidized business owners who pay less than a living wage, allowing them to keep good workers without raising their pay. Perhaps we should say that business owners are dependent on the government. On the other hand, some argue that receiving the EITC creates dependence on the part of the recipients. However, I'm not sure why dependence on our government—essentially our collective neighbors—is worse than dependence on our employer. In any case, the Christian image is not one of independence, but interdependence. We all depend on one another.

The Earned Income Tax Credit is, however, a necessity for many people with low wages. While the federal minimum wage is meant to ensure a baseline living for those who work, the current $7.25 an hour rate simply cannot do that. A full-time job at this wage pays $15,600 a year, barely enough to rent an apartment, let alone support a family in even the least expensive locations. Many states have set higher rates at or approaching $15 an hour. Even at this level, many family's struggle to find housing that takes up less than half of their income.

---

25. Earned income and Earned Income Tax Credit (EITC) tables, IRS, https://www.irs.gov/credits-deductions/individuals/earned-income-tax-credit/earned-income-and-earned-income-tax-credit-eitc-tables. Accessed February 9, 2025.

## If You Don't Work, You Don't Eat

Benefits such as TANF (direct cash assistance) and SNAP (commonly called food stamps) are limited to those who are working, disabled, or seeking work. These qualifications stem from our ingrained societal belief that people only deserve to eat if they are working. When we look back at the early church, they shared all they had in common so that everyone could eat. But Paul also writes to the Thessalonians and warns them to watch out for those who are not doing their share:

> Now concerning love of the brothers and sisters, you do not need to have anyone write to you, for you yourselves have been taught by God to love one another, and indeed you do love all the brothers and sisters throughout Macedonia. But we urge you, brothers and sisters, to do so more and more, to aspire to live quietly, to mind your own affairs, and to work with your hands, as we directed you, so that you may behave properly toward outsiders and be dependent on no one.—1 Thessalonians 4:9-12

Paul wants this new, countercultural church to look good to outsiders. He calls them to be unobtrusive—living quietly, staying out of one another's business, and getting to work. Since the church members were already dependent on one another and this familial dependence was a cultural norm, it seems likely that the directive to be "dependent on no one" (v. 12) is Paul's way of encouraging the church to find its support from within instead of asking outsiders for support. Paul's guidance continues in the second letter to the Thessalonians:

> Now we command you, brothers and sisters, in the name of our Lord Jesus Christ, to keep away from every brother or sister living irresponsibly and not according to the tradition that they received from us. For you yourselves know how

> you ought to imitate us; we were not irresponsible when we were with you, and we did not eat anyone's bread without paying for it, but with toil and labor we worked night and day so that we might not burden any of you. This was not because we do not have that right but in order to give you an example to imitate. For even when we were with you, we gave you this command: anyone unwilling to work should not eat. For we hear that some of you are living irresponsibly, mere busybodies, not doing any work. Now such persons we command and exhort in the Lord Jesus Christ to do their work quietly and to earn their own living. Brothers and sisters, do not be weary in doing what is right. Take note of those who do not obey what we say in this letter; have nothing to do with them, so that they may be ashamed. Do not regard them as enemies, but admonish them as brothers and sisters.—2 Thessalonians 3:6-15

The language is even stronger here. In verse 10, Paul insists that if you don't work then you don't eat. This verse could be read to mean paid work, and in verse 8, Paul emphasizes his own decision to work for pay. However, verses 6, 7, and 11 make it clear that the main issue is not income, but avoiding the damaging disorder and meddling brought about by those without something better to do. I imagine that it's similar to me telling my retired husband to get out of the house and out of my hair. "Find a job!" I'll holler. Paul wants the outsider's vision of the church to be one of order, not chaos. We can't do the work we need to do to take care of one another if there are people sticking their fingers in everything.

I highlight these texts because they are often used to argue that we should help only people who are working. People's arguments vary; many say we should include exemptions for people with disabilities, family care responsibilities, or those who have retired. Others argue it more straightforwardly: anyone not working should not eat.

In response, I'll note that no other biblical texts put limits on our care for the poor, the orphan, the widow, and the stranger. The judgment in the story of the sheep and the goats also suggests no tests are being imposed to see who truly qualifies as hungry, thirsty, or in need of clothing, healing, and visitation. This Lent, spend some time considering your views on this and working through some of these arguments. If, after this consideration, you find yourself convinced that only those who work should be helped, then I strongly encourage you to find even more ways to support the working poor.

Most people who are poor not only work, they work hard. It's a common myth that the people who work the hardest gain the most benefit from our economy. In fact, I'd argue the opposite is true. In terms of grueling labor, the people who use their hands and feet to feed us, clean our homes, gather our crops, lift our ill bodies, and cover the night shift are the people who make the least for their work. What should the reward be for this type of work? It certainly should not be anxiety, a fear of homelessness, and sickness brought about because of an inability to go to the doctor.

## Government Support for the Wealthy

Given the many objections offered against using the federal budget to help the poor, I have been surprised to learn how much financial support is provided to those who are middle-class or wealthy. Our mildly progressive tax system increases the tax rate for higher incomes, but this is often offset by subsidies that aren't easily noticed. In *Poverty by America*, Matthew Desmond demonstrates that those with the most money also receive the most government benefits. For example, healthcare premiums and retirement contributions are considered pre-tax income and are not taxed as salary. This quiet benefit personally saves me thousands of dollars a year while costing the federal government $1.8 trillion in foregone revenue.[26] The mortgage interest deduction and certain college savings plans are similarly structured benefits that provide advantages for those of us with excess to save. These benefits arrive through tax reductions rather than direct payments, obscuring the nature of their support.

Compare these benefits with the $1.1 trillion spent annually on welfare programs.[27] Note also that tax benefits flow directly to the individual filer, while much of the money spent on welfare programs goes to administrative costs and never reaches those who are poor.

## Redistribution of Wealth

While we should work to redistribute wealth within the small circle of our congregation, we could also try to do more through our city, state, and federal administrations. The federal government possesses unmatched capacity to collect resources nationwide and spread that wealth to the people who need it most. Our tax system transcends geographic boundaries, making it possible to channel resources from prosperous regions to struggling communities everywhere.

Many existing federal programs already demonstrate this principle. Both Temporary Aid for Needy Families (TANF) and the Supplemental Nutrition Assistance Program (SNAP) are funded federally, but distributed as block grants to states and tribes. TANF exists to assist families with children, and SNAP, along with school lunch programs, addresses food security. Both require recipients to work or prove that they cannot work. Medicaid, the government health insurance program for low-income Americans, combines federal and state funding alongside state administration. None of these programs—TANF, SNAP, and

26. Desmond, *Poverty By America,* 92.

27. Michael D. Tanner, "Poverty and Welfare" in *The 2022 Cato Handbook for Policymakers,* https://www.cato.org/sites/cato.org/files/2023-03/cato-handbook-9th-edition.pdf. Accessed January 19, 2025.

Medicaid—are available to undocumented immigrants, and even legal immigrants face various restrictions.

This patchwork system of federally-funded and state-managed safety nets means that we are gathering funds from workers nationwide, while allowing states to adjust distribution to local economic realities. Federal guidelines attempt to ensure consistency, while state administration theoretically provides regional flexibility. Critics who claim that the federal government ignores local needs misunderstand the system—states determine eligibility and benefit levels within federal parameters.

For most, the largest local wealth-sharing program is K-12 education. Schools depend primarily on local property taxes, with federal funds supporting special education, disability services, and meal programs. This leads to an uneven educational environment nationwide. Poor communities find themselves sending their students to underfunded schools, while those living in wealthy areas also get access to higher-grade education. Local control, however valuable, limits our ability to provide the best education to the largest number of students.

In the United States, our government is ultimately a reflection of us. The preamble of our Constitution insists that "we the people" created this government to "promote the general welfare" for all of us. We bear responsibility for expressing our views about what our government should do and electing leaders who share that vision. Therefore, we are accountable for how our government treats the most vulnerable among us.

One novel strategy for redistributing wealth is the concept of a Universal Basic Income (UBI). This approach—also called unconditional cash transfers—provides regular payments to citizens, regardless of income. Additionally, it is not means-tested, and there are no eligibility requirements, thus the term "universal." These payments are not necessarily enough to live on; instead, they serve as a safety net. A steady, dependable income increases the ability of people to make changes that will improve their lives over the long haul. With a basic income, it is easier to move somewhere with a lower cost of living, work part-time, go to school, or take care of childcare while you work. This stability breeds peace of mind and can lead to better long-term financial planning.

UBI pilot programs have also yielded encouraging results. In Stockton, California, 125 randomly selected residents received a check for $500 each month. Recipients reported spending the money on necessities—groceries, utilities, and vehicle repairs. Critics of such programs fear that UBI encourages wasteful spending, yet research from Stockton and similar studies found that almost none of the money is spent on things like tobacco or alcohol.[28]

Even if there were wasteful spending, our current welfare system also has its own waste in the form of costly paperwork and staff to both check for compliance and advise people on the rules of the program. A well-designed UBI plan would eliminate most of these costs by serving everyone equally. Eliminating some of the tax breaks provided to wealthier people could fund a UBI program at costs close to what we are presently spending, while delivering more cash to the people who need it most.

If this idea seems like a bridge too far, we could instead focus on expanding the Earned Income Tax Credit. Or we could direct our attention to increasing the tax rate paid in the top tax bracket or add another higher bracket. In 2024, married couples paid 37% in taxes for income *exceeding* $751,600. Historically, the top rate has been as high as 92% and was 70% until 1963.[29] Alternatively, we could seek to make high earners pay Social Security taxes on more of their income to keep this safety net funded well into the future.

---

28. Desmond, *Poverty By America*, 87.

29. As a reminder, tax rates only apply on income made above a certain dollar amount, not on a person's entire income. For instance, the 92% tax rate that existed in 1952 was applied to annual income above $300,000 (the equivalent of about $3.5 million dollars annually today).

Critics claim that wealthy people wouldn't pursue more prestigious jobs with more responsibility or jobs that are more intellectually stimulating if we taxed their top earnings at 70%, 80%, or 90%. I contend that it is quite unfair to wealthy people to assume that they—we—are motivated by money alone. Consider a $10,000 pay raise that pushes someone over the line into a hypothetical 70% bracket. While their existing income is taxed at the lower rates they've already been paying, they keep only $3,000 of the raise—roughly $1.44 per hour across the course of a year. I assure you that every poor person would gladly accept such a raise. Is it reasonable to think that this would somehow be inadequate for high earners?

## Tithing as Taxes

All of these social programs require funding from the middle-class and wealthy citizens through various taxes—income, property, and sales taxes, as well as capital gains and inheritance taxes. For those of us who are part of a congregation, we also tithe to our churches. However, most of us view these obligations as fundamentally different from one another.

Yet the concept of tithing emerged at a time when religious and government authority were one and the same. Tithes, mostly crops and livestock, were offered to these authorities both for their own material support and to allow them to redistribute resources to the poor. What we give to the church today is used for the cost of the building and to support the pastor, just as how the money we pay to the government is used for employees and buildings. And each, in its own way, uses some of these funds to care for the poor. What percent of your church's income is used to care for the poor? For some added context, about one-sixth (16%) of your federal tax payments go to support programs providing for those who are poor.[30]

We turn to the prophet Malachi to further illuminate this connection:

> Will anyone rob God? Yet you are robbing me! But you say, "How are we robbing you?" In your tithes and offerings! You are cursed with a curse, for you are robbing me—the whole nation of you! Bring the full tithe into the storehouse, so that there may be food in my house, and thus put me to the test, says the LORD of hosts; see if I will not open the windows of heaven for you and pour down for you an overflowing blessing.—Malachi 3:8-10

In this and other scriptures about tithing, God demands what belongs to God. Tithing is not voluntary; it is a commandment. All that we have is God's, and the nation collects a share so "there may be food in my house" (v. 10). God's house feeds priests, government workers, and the poor. Today, we call this a tax used to redistribute the wealth of the land. The result will ideally be an overflowing blessing.

Deuteronomy explicitly designates tithes for immigrants, orphans, and widows, alongside the priests. Payment of this tax-tithe results brings in a blessing on the nation:

> "Every third year you shall bring out the full tithe of your produce for that year and store it within your towns; the Levites, because they have no allotment or inheritance with you, as well as the resident aliens, the orphans, and the widows in your towns, may come and eat their fill so that

30. See Cato for $1.1 trillion spent annually on welfare programs compared to a federal budget of 6.8 trillion in 2024.

> the Lord your God may bless you in all the work that you undertake.—Deuteronomy 14:28-29

Many misinterpret Levitical guidelines about gleaning to be about voluntary charity. But Leviticus is establishing the *laws* of the nation. This is a progressive tax structure, a foundational tithe from everyone who has income, and an additional percentage paid by those with excess, that is, landowners, who must leave crops behind in their fields for the poorest to harvest. These people do not pay, but instead receive the benefit of these taxes:

> "When you reap the harvest of your land, you shall not reap to the very edges of your field or gather the gleanings of your harvest. You shall not strip your vineyard bare or gather the fallen grapes of your vineyard; you shall leave them for the poor and the alien: I am the Lord your God.
> —Leviticus 19:9-10

Does thinking about your taxes as a kind of tithe affect how you think about taxes? While there is certainly a large share going to other things, some of which are of questionable value or importance, some is going to benefit the common good. Does this theological framework make you feel better about paying them?

## Taxes as Sharing

Here's one idea we can try to change the mentality around wealth that doesn't cost anything (except possibly public ridicule): celebrate paying taxes. Yes, seriously.

Our culture expects tax complaints. We frame taxes as burdens; in some circles, they're explicitly referred to as theft. Progressives complain about money wasted on tax breaks for the wealthy, while those who are more conservative object to funds that support the "undeserving." But all across the political spectrum, everyone dislikes paying taxes.

Should we seek tax reductions? Taxes distribute the costs of government services and support across the whole society. We pay taxes to support the common good. While it's appropriate to critique how money is spent, sharing wealth with our neighbors through taxes is a good thing. For Christians, paying taxes helps us in some small way live out our obligation to care for our neighbors.

History demonstrates the power of collective taxation. Once, only wealthy families were able to afford a good education and often only for their sons. Then we dreamed up the idea of universal public education. Communities pooled their local funds and made schooling a reality for all. Then there are all the other services that are difficult, if not impossible, to maintain individually, such as military defense, fire departments, and public libraries. Similarly, efforts to redistribute food, housing, and healthcare are more effective when spread over a wider population.

I recently attended a church event that required an overnight stay at a hotel. Since it was church business, we had a certificate showing that we were exempt from the taxes typically collected by the hotel. Hotel taxes, paid mostly by vacationers and business travelers, are especially high. It was certainly nice to pay less money, but what does it mean when someone from a church says that they choose not to pay this tax. While it's certainly legal, it also suggests that we do not want to fund the common good. What if we instead proclaimed, both to ourselves and others, "Yes, I would like to pay that tax. I would like to contribute to the common good through this tax."

I once knew a couple who moved from the suburbs outside Washington, D.C., to a small town in Iowa. Their modest townhouse in Washington sold for such a high price that they felt it was "required" for them to splurge on a huge four-bedroom colonial for their new home. They have no children, so I wondered what they meant when they said it was "required." The answer? They wanted to avoid the capital gains tax. If you don't roll over the profit from the sale of your home into a new home, then you have to pay a tax on the profit.

But why resist paying taxes on money that came from simply living in a house that appreciated in value? Why is that something to avoid? What have we done to *deserve* the increased value of our homes? Unlike taxes on our wages, there is no claim here that we worked hard to earn this money. We've made an investment in real estate, lived in that investment, and lucked out when the property grew in value. This is a win! Why not gladly pay the 15% or 20% tax on what was gained? For that matter, why shouldn't capital gains taxes be 50%? 75%? While we're at it, let's increase the taxes on lottery winnings as well!

Spiritual poverty reminds us that God owns the land. When we come out ahead as a result of caring for our share, we should be grateful. When it is time to sell, we can embrace the opportunity to contribute to the common good.

## How Do We Change the System?

In a democracy, voting remains our number one tool for changing the system. We must ask ourselves which candidates will act on our ideals and advance our values of caring for the poor, treating all people equally, and helping to lift up the oppressed. We aren't always faced with ideal choices, or even good choices. All candidates for office are imperfect, as are we, but Christians must vote with their faith and their vision of a better world guiding their choices.

While churches cannot (and perhaps should not) endorse specific candidates, we can help members of our congregations figure out how their own Christian values come into play for each electoral race. In local races, examine how school and municipal policies affect the poorest among us. Quality schooling proves especially important for those lacking material resources. Additionally, children struggle to learn when they are not able to eat both breakfast and lunch. For state and federal elections, encourage your community to support people who will prioritize care for those who are poor.

It is important to know how the biblical witness informs our viewpoints and our vote. Micah 6:8 calls us to do justice, love kindness, and walk humbly before God. Humility demands listening to others; kindness points to direct service and charity, and justice requires standing up for those who need our support. As we have discussed throughout this book, the biblical witness is firmly on the side of redistributing material resources so that the poor get a fair share of what is God's.

Between elections, communicate your values and priorities to your elected officials. We must abandon the view that representatives who disagree with us are not truly our representatives. When addressing representatives who identify as Christians, it is particularly valuable to share the biblical witness behind our beliefs that caring for the poor and the oppressed is how we best serve God.

Encourage members of your community to contact politicians by email, fax, mail, and, whenever possible, by phone or in person. If they choose to use a script when calling, invite them to add a line or two that is specific to them, specific to your congregation, or specific to your faith. It's good and helpful when we share stories about someone who is struggling and how the legislation under consideration will either help or hurt them. Beyond this, work to build relationships with decision makers at the local, state, and federal level. Invite them to meet people who need the resources that the government can provide.

When it comes to meeting with politicians face-to-face, there are three common approaches. First, you can schedule an appointment to visit yourself. This is straightforward and allows you to address your primary issues and concerns one on one. Second, you can participate in a legislative action day focused around a particular issue that you care about. These include learning sessions about the topic, which sometimes are followed by pre-arranged meetings with legislators or their aids.

Finally, the third and most powerful option is to schedule a visit with your representative as a congregation. While this is rarely done, it has the potential to create significant change. Invite three or four people to represent your congregation during the meeting and make it clear that they are representing your entire church community. If you are meeting with an elected official who is Christian, bring a written, one-page biblical argument concerning the issue at hand. Also, be prepared to share a few personal stories about how the proposed legislation will affect people in your congregation or people your congregation works with. Imagine the things you might achieve if you could get three or four other congregations to do the same!

You can also help those who run for office by explaining the background behind your community's faith-based opinions on the treatment of those who are poor. Furthermore, you can foster dialogue around how to build a culture that includes a collective responsibility to care for one another. As Christians, our engagement with public officials transcends partisan loyalty and demonstrates our love of one another. We are called to engage lovingly and firmly, making sure our officials understand the deeply felt consequences of these programs and policies. Our goal is to get to know our leaders as people and help them to transform.

Political action can also be economic in nature. Churches can organize the membership to engage in national or local consumer boycotts and "No Buy Days." Find one volunteer to regularly research local businesses and pass this information on to the whole congregation so that they can get involved. Be sure to inform the company you are boycotting what you want them to do differently—pay a living wage, offer healthcare benefits, treat low-wage employees respectfully, and so on. Businesses are influenced by spending decisions.

Perhaps the most visible form of political action is the protest. Protests provide public witness against unjust policies and decisions. One group near me organized stand-outs after hearing about the heckling of immigrants at nearby shelters. They stood with signs and slogans with scripture about the care of strangers in front of the shelter to make sure the residents, and hecklers, knew that many in the community supported them.

If possible, protest together as a congregation.[31] Protesting with your congregation together is a powerful experience. Wear t-shirts or make other signs that identify your congregation and encourage people who are ordained to wear collars or stoles. Your church can choose to be a voice of moral authority! It's also important to make arrangements ahead of time about what to do if someone is separated from the group.

---

31. If you and your church decide to join a protest, connect with others and make a plan about what to do in the face of violence. Decide whether you will stay or leave, where will you meet, and, if you stay, your strategy for getting legal help. If there are arrests planned, the people involved will have had training in advance of the event—don't join them unless you were part of the training. Whether or not you are willing to be arrested, consider taking nonviolent protest training before protesting.

## LENTEN REFLECTIONS

### A DAILY PRAYER FOR THE SIXTH WEEK OF LENT

Holy God, help us to see the world as you created it to be. Open our eyes to the opportunities to bring about justice and the ways that we can change both our communities and the entire world for the better. Give us the strength to act with focus, dedication, and passion as we seek to do good in your name. Amen.

### SIXTH WEEK OF LENT

#### MONDAY REFLECTIONS • Research What Is Already Happening

Research what your council of churches or ecumenical council is working on in your area. Research secular organizations that assist people who are poor. What services are available? Where are there gaps? Are there any places where you can give money directly to poor people? Are they places you can volunteer, or are they primarily places to send money? What is their mission, and do they get at root causes?

#### TUESDAY REFLECTIONS • Choose a Focus

What is the one topic your congregation, or you as a Christian, would focus your work on? Immigration? Disability? Prison? Homelessness? Affordable housing? Food accessibility? Employment assistance? A living wage? Support for people leaving prison?

#### WEDNESDAY REFLECTIONS • Politics

Churches are permitted to stand up for issues and to engage in theological analysis about political things, but not to be partisan. Does your church engage the political sphere? How do you walk the line to avoid partisanship? What are topics your members care about?

## THURSDAY REFLECTIONS • Work to Eat?

Should people who don't work not be able to eat? What are your arguments for or against this? How can you explain your view to someone who doesn't agree? What about people who are wealthy or who are retired? What types of supports are reasonable for people with disabilities?

## FRIDAY REFLECTIONS • Protest

Does your church engage in mild protests like pride marches, hunger walks, and the like? What would it take to expand that involvement? How many from your church would attend a protest? How can this be a ministry of the church? Do you see a place for engaging in more controversial forms of protest? Is it possible that the original Palm Sunday was a protest of sorts? A cry for justice?

## SATURDAY REFLECTIONS • Pick an Issue

Research a systemic issue you care about. Do the poor have access to banking systems? How well does the minimum wage work in your area, and how much are most businesses paying their lowest-paid workers? What is the history of taxing generational wealth? What are the rules in your town, county, or state that prevent providing sufficient affordable housing? If there is plenty of housing, what helped make that happen? Find out how a person qualifies for disability and how much the payment would be. Research the difference between SSI and SSDI benefits. You might also consider researching a topic such as disability or immigration status and how that affects poverty and wealth.

## PALM SUNDAY REFLECTIONS • Celebrate

Imagine Jesus entering into the city of Jerusalem with people shouting. If you were there, what would you be excited about? At that moment in the city, what would be your hope for you and your people? What can you celebrate now about Jesus' message and Jesus' life? How have you or your church affected the community around you? What systems-change project have you or your church engaged in? How did it go? What part of that work are you proudest of?

# INTERLUDE

## Church-Based Justice Projects

Housing, food insecurity, and healthcare stand as the three biggest issues for people who are poor. Childcare costs, support for people with disabilities, immigrant services, and elder care are also significant issues related to poverty and compound the three core issues mentioned previously. There are also several groups that are particularly vulnerable to poverty, including youth aging out of foster care, people leaving prison, and people with mental health challenges. As a church, choose where you will focus your attention based on the connections you already have. From this starting point, begin to build networks, branching out from the people you know.

Partner with organizations that are already working to bring about systemic change. Your denomination likely coordinates some of these efforts already. For instance, in 2019, the United Church of Christ teamed up with RIP Medical Debt to eliminate more than $100 million in medical debt and aims to eventually pay off more than $500 million. You and your congregation can be a part of this work! In the business world, collection agencies buy debt at a discount and then work to collect the amount due as a profit-making enterprise. Organizations like RIP Medical Debt eliminate this debt by buying it from hospitals and billing agencies, often for as little as ten cents on the dollar and forgiving that debt instead.[32] This is only one example of a tangible way that your congregation can help those living in poverty.

32. Check out https://unduemedicaldebt.org/ to get involved.

## Poor People's Campaign

Your church can also participate in advocacy work and protest movements like the one I described earlier. The Poor People's' Campaign continues to do work today in the tradition of the work done by Martin Luther King, Jr. His vision of Black and white people working together for peace as well as both racial and economic justice represented a countercultural challenge to social norms. And that vision was steeped in the Christian conviction that we all are God's people together.

It remains difficult to convince political candidates to seriously address poverty. Both political parties prefer to emphasize the needs of the middle class. In the face of this challenge, the Poor People's Campaign uses a faith-based approach to unify people around all of the ways those living in poverty are treated badly. The campaign calls for a higher minimum wage as well as public recognition and stronger policies to respond to the discrimination faced by Black and Brown people in schooling and at work. They push for protections for immigrants and advocate for the government to address environmental disasters that are disastrous for those who are poor. The campaign also works to register poor people to vote and to get these voters to the polls. While they do not support any individual candidates, they take a strong stand on issues that affect people who are poor.

Your congregation can support the Poor People's Campaign through financial contributions, by building relationships with people living in poverty in your own community, and by using campaign resources for voter registration and mobilization. The organization operates through local chapters that plan and take local actions, all coordinated alongside the national organization. Once a year, everyone gathers in Washington D.C. and in other cities to advocate for the poor together with one voice.[33]

These are only a few examples of tangible ways that your congregation can help those living in poverty.

33. Find out more about the Poor People's Campaign at www.poorpeoplescampaign.org.

7

# Connections

## My Story

Church has always been the place where I learned how to think about and serve those who are poor. As a child in elementary school, I would collect coins during Lent in a milk carton decorated like a rabbit. The coins were to help our church project that was raising money for "Bunnies for Bolivia" through the Heifer Project. (Heifer provides rabbits to poor families as a food source.)

Church is where we sponsored Vietnamese immigrants and talked about work opportunities for people who have nothing. And newly on my own, church is where I first worked at a homeless shelter. It was at the shelter that I first began to question how the *way* we give matters. I was uncomfortable with the way we required women at the shelter to ask for sanitary supplies: "How many and what size?" Despite concerns that someone might take "too many," I worked to change the system to allow each person to take what they wanted.

In those early years as a working adult, my spouse and I struggled with our own finances—with minimum wage jobs and part-time teaching, we barely got by. My reaction at that time was mostly anger rather than helping to make a difference.

But I *was* angry about poverty, and I *did* want to change the world. I took part in Habitat for Humanity blitz builds (building a neighborhood in a week!) and voted for refugee-supporting candidates. I learned about poverty from my own experiences, from coworkers' stories, from the women I met at the shelter, and from study. Sermons and Bible studies informed my worldview.

Over the years as my own wealth grew, my theology also deepened. I've developed a more mature understanding of how we can share together rather than simply identify as either givers or receivers. In the process of this discovery, I stopped overworking and decided to attend seminary. I felt more and more that church can be a force for change and that my relationship with God is what drives my concern for the poor.

I went to Episcopal Divinity School in Cambridge, Massachusetts, for a curriculum that focused on racism, classism, sexism, how theology can either support or resist oppression, and how to be a church that is engaged with the world. It was a highlight experience full of answers for everything! And then I was called to a church that closed. And *then* I got divorced. I was poor and struggling once again, and the work of getting the church engaged in the world seemed much harder.

But I'd developed a vision of what church can be, and after working a short time at common cathedral, a street church in Boston, I copied the idea by creating Worcester Fellowship in central Massachusetts along with a seminary friend. There, as our relationships with homeless and poor parishioners grew, we discovered how much they wanted to be givers themselves. In response, I read about ministries where food-insecure individuals led the food distribution and meal programs and served as volunteers. Despite facing struggles with everything from mental health to addictions to loneliness to just showing up on time, these volunteers created successful programs that addressed the real needs of people just like them. Nearly everyone, it turns out, prefers giving to receiving. (See my book *Five Loaves, Two Fish, Twelve Volunteers: Growing a Relational Food Ministry* for more on that.)

Writing, for me, is the key to figuring out what I believe, so *this* book has changed my perspective again—on God, on poverty, and importantly, on my own access to excess money. My husband and I revised our wills. We've decided to leave modest amounts to family members who are living on the edge and struggling financially, but have also chosen to direct most of what we have to organizations working to make the world better for all those who are poor. We've also reworked our budget to increase the amount we give now. Despite these decisions, and despite my efforts to trust God, I'm still really nervous about health insurance and our own financial security. I worry about what will happen if we run out of money. I want to believe that we can celebrate and share generously with one another in the midst of our anxiety about money. I want to remember and embody Jesus' life of trust when facing uncertainty and taking risks.

## Maundy Thursday

The story of the Last Supper shows us Jesus choosing celebration and the presence of friends in the moments right before facing the worst that life can offer. I find it difficult to emulate this kind of trust, this trust that God is with us through hard times. I want to be the type of person who looks risk and fear in the eye and responds with a party.

John 13:1-17 describes Jesus washing the disciples' feet. Whether or not your congregation practices foot washing on Maundy Thursday, this passage is a useful one to meditate on when talking to your community about the difficulty of accepting help. In this story, Jesus assumes the role of a servant, cleansing the day's dust and grime from the feet of his followers, who are also his friends and people he loves. We never learn if the other disciples shared Peter's discomfort with this, but he is the one who openly protests.

It's tempting to interpret Peter's objection to the propriety of the situation, believing that washing feet was beneath Jesus' dignity. We think that Peter must have simply believed that Jesus was too important for servanthood. However, I encourage us to notice our own resistance to receiving help. We feel like we shouldn't need it. We don't want it. This scripture offers us the opportunity to acknowledge our needs and accept that God is calling us to let others provide for those needs. The disciples were more than capable of washing their own feet, but that's not the point. Letting someone else provide for us can be a deeply spiritual experience, drawing us closer to God through humility. Perhaps this ritual symbolizes all the ways that we can deepen our connection to God by receiving help from others.

## Circle of Mission

There's still a lot of work to be done to address poverty in the United States. As Christians, we bear responsibility for acknowledging this challenge and identifying ways that we can be part of this work. As we've journeyed through Lent, I hope you've reflected on how you've responded to wealth and poverty in the past and developed some new ideas about how you want to engage the issue in future—as an individual and collectively with your church community.

In my mind, charity work and justice work are not two ends of a spectrum. Instead, they form a circle together. Practicing one naturally leads to the other.

For people who have excess, anti-poverty work typically begins by writing checks and funding organizations and ministries from a distance. Curiosity naturally follows, and this person might try to learn more about the organization or perhaps visit the ministry. After sending a few donations, perhaps they volunteer a few hours. They take a Saturday and sort food at the pantry, help a family move, or accompany an immigrant to an appointment. Gradually, the commitment to this work and these people deepens. If they spend as much time meeting people in need as they do cooking or sorting donations, then relationships will start to grow and the ministry will feel even more important. The ministry becomes personal. This person, who initially just wrote a check, is no longer giving but sharing, receiving as much as they provide to the ministry themselves. This is the ideal trajectory for someone who gives out of their excess.

Through direct service, we get to know people. We hear their stories and witness first-hand the systemic barriers they face. We start to see all the effort people put into improving their situations, only to be rebuffed time after time. When the obvious solutions don't work or don't work enough, we begin to recognize the injustice of the situation.

In response, we look for the next step. Perhaps we plan to join in a legislative action day or listen to a learning session about the day-to-day challenges faced by those who are poor. A prison ministry has an educational event about the school-to-prison pipeline devastating Black and Brown communities. A food bank screens a documentary about food waste or about the role of immigrant labor in farmwork. Homeless advocates testify at the state house about foster youth aging out of the system into a life of homelessness. We learn more and more, and we begin to see the system's failures directly.

Our knowledge grows, and it changes us. As a person understands more about both the issues involved and the people struggling within this system, systemic solutions themselves become urgent and personal. Nobody randomly chooses to be passionate about an issue of social justice. We advocate in the places where we've witnessed systemic dysfunction. We fight for the people we care about who we have seen hurt. We meet people. We learn more. We love more and we do more.

I used to say that people can either give money or give time, but my experience has been the opposite. The people who spend time in the ministry tend to be the same people who give the most money. Volunteering leads people to give money, and giving money leads to volunteering. The people who have been doing charity find themselves wanting to change the system. And then the circle continues, as those engaged in making change find that they want to give more of both their time and money to support the important work being done.

In the cooperative board game *Pandemic* (which I played weekly until there was a real pandemic), the winning strategy requires finding a delicate balance between healing individuals in a given city and spending resources finding a cure. If you don't heal anyone, the illness can spread into the next city, but if you spend all your time healing people, you won't find the cure to save the entire world and win the game. Essentially, you've got to provide charity while also working for justice.

This balance is evident in food ministries, for example. We need to expand SNAP benefits and remove the barriers that keep those who qualify from applying for the benefits they're eligible for. But while we work on making these necessary systemic changes, people still need to eat. This is where our food pantries and meal programs come in. These programs are essential for meeting today's needs. The same is true for housing, mental health services, immigration services, and more. There's a lot of systemic change to make, but in the meantime, we meet the needs that exist today. Our relationships with those who are poor continue to drive us through the circle of mission.

## A Story

My cousin Sylvia is well-educated. She can think for herself, and she can take care of herself too, thank you very much. When I told her I was working on this book, she was quick to explain that I have poverty all wrong. Then, she told me this story.

When Sylvia was younger—around forty years old—she was attending college while raising two young children. She was pinching pennies to get along, and she was also scared for her kids.

One day, her bank incorrectly charged her a $3 fee. (How long ago were bank fees $3?!?) That may not sound like a lot, but for Sylvia, $3 was significant. She talked to a bank teller, and the teller argued the bank's point of view, appealed to bank policy, and insisted that the fee wasn't such a big deal. But it was a big deal to Sylvia! It mattered to her.

What was most offensive to Sylvia, and what still had her upset when I visited recently, is that the teller did not see Sylvia—the person standing right in front of her—as a person who mattered. That's what she really wanted. She wanted to be seen and to be acknowledged as a person who matters.

Once the problem presented itself, the teller had the opportunity to create a relationship. As part of that relationship, Sylvia and the teller would be addressing the $3 fee together. Even today, Sylvia suggests that she might have misunderstood why she was being charged a fee. Maybe the teller was correct; maybe Sylvia was wrong. Two people in a relationship can figure things out; they can work out if a mistake happened, if the policy should be more flexible, or find a solution that meets both their needs.

But the teller did not try to create that relationship. She could not imagine anything other than following policy. Why is that? Is it because Sylvia is a woman? Is it because she's Hispanic? Short? Blue-eyed? Or was it because Sylvia had very little money in the bank? I don't know. Maybe it was a combination of these reasons, or maybe it was none of them at all. Maybe the teller was just having a bad day.

What I do know is that Sylvia's problem was not *just* poverty. She was also confronting the way we push people aside rather than engage them as friends, as neighbors, and as, well, people.

Failure to create relationships doesn't follow a particular politics either. People who want reforms to banking practices so that the poor are not charged unreasonable fees are just as likely to overlook Sylvia as those who feel that she deserves to pay these fees and more.

## Relationships and Solidarity

However we choose to respond to poverty, we must do it by creating and building relationships. We believe in a God who is not a distant creator, but nearby and in relationship with us. The strength of church is our ability to be in relationship with God and with one another.

During Lent, we draw close to God in church and in our weekly studies. We meet God through reading our Bible and engaging in spiritual practices. We look within ourselves and search for spiritual poverty. Amid all of this, we must not forget that Christ is found in the poor. For most of us, and often in Lent, we search only within the confines of the church and our traditions. But Jesus tells the sheep and the goats that he is the one who is hungry, thirsty, and naked. He is the stranger, the sick, and the person in prison. To learn about Christ is to learn from people in need; to be close to Christ is to be close to those in need, and to care for Christ is to care for those who need care. Whether we are rich or poor, have excess or not enough, spiritual poverty drives us closer to one another and closer to God in the process.

Thus, we cannot do ministry *to* or *for* others. We must instead figure out how to do ministry *with* others. Each of us must be willing to give *and* be willing to receive. If we are we willing to give advice, are we also willing to receive it? If we are we willing to accompany our neighbor somewhere, are we also willing to invite a neighbor to come with us? Are we willing to take risks to our own well-being to share more fully with others?

Our ministries need to meet people's material needs, but perhaps the most important thing we do in Christian ministry is building relationships—getting to know people, hear their stories, and listen for their underlying cravings and desires. The ministry of saying "God loves you" and "You are important" is incredibly undervalued. This is evangelism. This is good news! This is the way we proclaim that we value others, that we value our relationships with them, and that we see their value as God's children.

In the end, we want to have a deep enough relationship with others that we find ourselves helping naturally. We want to discover ourselves helping each person because we understand that to help the other is help us all. This is solidarity. Solidarity is not just knowledge about those who are poor, but the fullness of life from the big to the small—from the worship services to the parties to helping to clean each other's homes. In true solidarity, I offer what I have, and I accept the gift that the other offers to me.

We each engage the world with our own understanding of poverty. We each develop our own understanding of what to do about it. With this in mind, each individual and each church must find a balance for how poverty, wealth, and our Christian life will intersect.

## The Servant Song

The Christian faith begins with the presumption that we see one another—and see Christ in one another.

We talked in the chapter on spiritual poverty about the importance of accepting help. It turns out that this is hard to do, and it's not a common theme in our music either. However, *The Servant Song,* a hymn by Richard Gillard, gets at this mutuality. It starts with the idea of me serving you, the needy, but switches immediately to the reality that you also might serve me:

> Will you let me be your servant,
> Let me be as Christ to you;
> Pray that I may have the grace to
> Let you be my servant, too.[34]

A true Christian ministry is one where we share the roles of giver and receiver.

---

34. Richard Gillard, "The Servant Song," in *The Faith We Sing* (Nashville: Abingdon Press, 2000), hymn 2222.

## What We Have Is God's

A brief summary of this entire book could simply be that all we have is God's. God created this world and the wealth that is in it. We are meant to share this wealth. There are two important callings for Christians that emerge as a result: 1) those who have more than average should choose to share, and 2) those who have less than average should accept their share.

How we choose to share is not always clear. Some may choose to share through acts of charity, some by funding work for significant systemic change, and some by paying their fair share in taxes. Some of us are part of churches that do hands-on work to redistribute wealth in our immediate community, and some are part of churches that advocate for long-term improvements in the way we distribute wealth in our town, our state, and our nation.

Working to alleviate poverty also includes working to improve the lot of those who are immigrants, fighting against racism, striving to make childcare affordable, and making efforts to improve schools serving those who are poor. Other efforts for justice also fall into this vein. Disability rights, for instance, is very much an anti-poverty effort, as is prison reform.

It is easy to be concerned that what we do is not enough. It is certainly true that no individual alone has the resources or the power to definitively "solve" poverty on their own. Nevertheless, it is still our responsibility to try. And sometimes a moderate amount can make a big difference.

## What Good Is $10,000?

Early in my ministry, I thought that winning $10,000 in a lottery was a small gain. Not that it's not a lot of money, but it didn't seem like enough to solve the problems of homelessness. I assumed that it would take a much larger investment to make any kind of difference.

Poverty felt so big, the system so overbearing, that it all felt overwhelming. I really wanted big solutions to homelessness.

I still want those big, systemic solutions. At the same time, working in ministry with people who have few material resources has taught me that a modest amount of money can make a huge difference in many people's lives.

Think about what you would do with $10,000. It's enough for first and last month's rent and a security deposit for an apartment. There's probably enough left over to furnish the place too. For someone with a steady income, that's just enough to meet their rent; a one-time influx of even $5,000 would be the difference between homelessness and having a place to live.

With $10,000, a person on a fixed income could decide to move to a different part of the country with a lower cost of living. It also costs approximately $10,000 for ten days of inpatient care at McLean Hospital, a psychiatric hospital in Massachusetts. Ten thousand dollars covers about two weeks of inpatient addiction rehab.

We often hear stories of massive medical debts. While three million people owe more than $10,000, about 85% owe between $250 and $10,000.[35] The average amount of credit card debt in the United States was $6,492 in 2025.[36] Imagine what $10,000 would do for any of the people in these situations.

For those of us who have enough material resources to cover our needs, how hard would it be to give up $10,000? Perhaps it would take a couple of years to save that much to give away. Perhaps you

35. Rakshit, Shameek, et al., *The Burden of Medical Debt in the United States,* Peterson-KFF Health System Tracker, https://www.healthsystemtracker.org/brief/the-burden-of-medical-debt-in-the-united-states. Accessed October 3, 2025.

36. Saks Frankel, Robin, "How Does Your Debt Compare? U.S. Average Credit Card Debt in the 2025," *Forbes*, September 10, 2025, https://www.forbes.com/advisor/credit-cards/average-credit-card-debt. Accessed October 3, 2025.

could write a check for it right now. Many churches could probably raise $10,000 in a month or two or even a few days if people were excited by the project. Maybe you could raise $10,000 every year, each time giving it to help a different person or small group of people.

It turns out that $10,000, a relatively modest amount in the grand scheme of things, can really make a difference.

## Concluding Thoughts

We've read the story of the sheep and the goats that insists we will be judged only on how we have cared for the poor. This story can be read as a story about charity, and it can also be read as a story about justice, but it is definitely a call to action. It requires that we see Christ in all of those who are in need.

We've also been reminded again and again that all we have is God's. Can we open our eyes and see that caring for the poor is about sharing God's wealth rather than hanging on to the things that feel like they belong to us? Caring for those who are poor is also about listening to those who are poor and empowering them to ask for what they deserve. We are all dependent on God to be our refuge, strength, and support. We can trust that God will be with us. We must be humble in our work, knowing that we don't have all the answers and that we cannot solve all the problems ourselves.

God offers blessings to those who are poor in spirit and woe to those who are rich. We have a choice about what to do with that information. What will we do?

# LENTEN REFLECTIONS

## A DAILY PRAYER FOR HOLY WEEK

Holy one, help us to see you. To see your strength, your witness, your courage, and your suffering. Help us to recognize the pain in people in our community. Help us to not look away. Guide us in the work to truly be the body of Christ in the world. Forgive us for the ways we fail to have the courage to change. Holy one, help us to see you in all whom we meet. Amen.

## HOLY WEEK

### MONDAY OF HOLY WEEK

During Jesus' time in Jerusalem, he preaches and teaches, but what I remember most is when he drives the money changers out of the Temple. I believe he was protecting the poor from dishonest business practices, but there are many interpretations of this story. Does this story affect your relationship to money or the relationship between money and church? Does your congregation offer opportunities to talk about Christian faith and money, or is it a taboo topic? How often is there preaching about money in your worship services? Were you taught to avoid talking about money and religion when you were growing up?

### TUESDAY OF HOLY WEEK

Later this week, we will hear much about Jesus' clothes. He will be dressed as a king and then stripped naked. Soldiers will divide his clothing among them. These are the last of his possessions to be taken. For funerals, sometimes the deceased is buried in their favorite clothing. Which of your clothes are most meaningful to you? What would you do with only your clothes? How are your clothes an important part of your life? What story do your clothes tell about you?

## WEDNESDAY OF HOLY WEEK

We've talked a lot about how everything belongs to God. What does it feel like to consider this truth? Do you believe it? Does it feel like a welcome admission? What does it make you feel? Why? How can you simultaneously acknowledge that everything belongs to God while honoring the hard work you have done? How do we balance the idea that all we have is a gift from God with our own effort?

## MAUNDY THURSDAY

On Maundy Thursday, we celebrate and remember the Last Supper. Jesus knew the risks when he chose to enter Jerusalem. He faces arrest, but amid this crisis, he shares a feast with his followers. What are your initial thoughts when envisioning this celebratory meal? Is this something you could see yourself doing? How does this experience show vulnerability? How does it show community? What does it mean to choose joy when confronting something frightening and unjust?

## GOOD FRIDAY

We started this study with ashes reminding us of death. Some say that the root of all fears is ultimately the fear of death. What do you think about this statement? Do you believe this to be true? We have talked a lot in this book about giving away what you have or, alternatively, being more willing to accept gifts and government support. Both are risky decisions. Does it make you afraid to give too much away? Does it make you afraid to rely on others for support? Why?

Do you believe that these fears are in some ways about death and loss? What does it say about us that we need others to support us?

## HOLY SATURDAY

On the day after the crucifixion, the disciples are hiding. They are overwhelmed by their grief and waiting to be arrested themselves. Some of the women who followed Jesus are waiting to go to the tomb to anoint the body. Everyone is waiting. Sometimes it feels that we as a nation are waiting to discover a way to deal with poverty. We are hoping that someone will just figure out the solution. Maybe someone will just do it for us or give us the guidance we need to deal with poverty in a new way. What does it mean to be waiting for something like this? What are we called to do during these moments of waiting? What are we waiting for?

## EASTER SUNDAY

How does the Resurrection change your view of what we should do about poverty? What does the Resurrection tell us about how to respond to poverty? Does it offer us a new way to encounter the world? Does it offer us hope for a better future? I imagine that most of you who have worked through this entire study have at least one thing in mind that you hope to do differently. What is that one thing? How will doing that one thing help you celebrate the Resurrection? How will it help you renew and restore things the way God intended them to be?

## GOOD FRIDAY

This Good Friday service is designed to center the suffering of the poor in your local community. It transforms the traditional Stations of the Cross, which mark the moments of Jesus' suffering, into a pilgrimage through your community and the places that mark the struggles of those who are poor in your world.[37]

In advance of this ritual, you will need to map out the locations where harm has happened in your community or where it continues to happen. In anticipation of this service, gather news stories from the previous year. Investigate stories about fires, violence, and other tragedies in your community. If you need additional locations, consider places like your local police station, fire station, food pantries, Social Security offices, subsidized housing, or even a local prison. You may find it helpful for your version of this practice to highlight immigrants or those living with disabilities. It's also possible to broaden this practice further to include more everyday sites like a laundromat, an apartment complex, a senior-living facility, a fast food restaurant, or a library.

If your participants will be driving between sites, choose only two or three. If you are walking around the neighborhood, then perhaps six to eight options within a reasonable distance would be suitable. Adapt this to your context.

At each location, gather, pray, remember, share, and then bless the site. Some of the sites may be especially poignant opportunities for people to share their memories of people or events at associated with that site. Provide them with the opportunity to add these remembrances.

---

37. The idea for this Good Friday liturgy comes from The Welcome Church, a street ministry in Philadelphia, PA, https://www.thewelcomechurch.org.

# STATIONS OF THE CROSS COMMUNITY WORSHIP

## FIRST STATION

*Start at either your church or one of your chosen sites.*

Read Psalm 22, or use this responsive adaptation of selections from the Psalm.

One: My God, my God, why have your forsaken us?

All: **Yet is was you who took us from the womb; you kept us safe on our mother's breast.**

One: O my God, we cry by day, but you do not answer; and by night, we find no rest.

All: **Since our mothers bore us, you have been our God.**

One: We are poured out like water; all our bones are out of joint.

All: **Yet you are holy, enthroned in the praises of your people.**

One: Our hearts are like wax; it is melted in our breasts.

All: **You do not hide your face from us, but hear when we cry out.**

One: O Lord, do not be far away! O help, come quickly to my aid.

All: **The poor and afflicted shall eat and be satisfied. May our hearts live forever!**

## HYMN

*Move to the next site.*

### AT EACH SITE

One: Let us gather together in the memory of those whose lives were disrupted by [event/ongoing events] that took/take place here [on date/each day]. Let us pray.

All: **Holy God, we are weeping with those who have lost so much. Hold them close. Help us to be a people who rise up to meet the needs of our neighbors. Be with our community as we struggle. Amen.**

*At each site, include the "Share" option if there are people who were present or who knew those involved.*

### SHARE

One: We ask you to lift up your memories of this place.

*People may share stories.*

*Offer the Litany of Remembering.*

### LITANY OF REMEMBERING

*Adjust this to match the circumstances of your site. Some samples are provided:*

### REMEMBER A FIRE

We remember this fire that started in the middle of the night. My God, my God, why have you forsaken us? *Silence.*

We remember the firefighters who came here to help us. [Add names of those who were injured.] *Silence.*

We remember the families who lost their housing this night. [Add names of people connected to your congregation who were displaced.] *Silence.*

We remember the people who lost their lives that night. [Add names of those who died.] *Silence.*

We trust that God does not hide their face from us, but hears when we cry out.

## REMEMBER FAMILY VIOLENCE OR AN OVERDOSE

We remember this family that was caught up in violence [or addiction.] My God, my God, why have you forsaken us? *Silence.*

We remember [names of specific individuals involved].

We remember the police who came here to help. [Or that the police were not able to help.] *Silence.*

We pray for all families that are experiencing violence [or addiction]. We trust that God does not hide their face from us, but hears when we cry out.

## REMEMBER AN ACCIDENT

We remember this family and the accident that has marred their lives forever. My God, my God, why have you forsaken us? *Silence.*

We remember [names of specific individuals involved].

We remember the police who came here to help. [Or that the police were not able to help.] *Silence.*

We pray for all families that are experiencing violence. We trust that God does not hide their face from us, but hears when we cry out.

## BLESSING

*Everyone is invited to lift their hands in blessing.*

One: God of healing, bless this space so that the memory of what happened here might be a call to action to care for all. Guide us to be a people who create change in our community and bring your love into the world.

All: **Amen.**

*Move to next site.*

## AT THE LAST SITE

*Add this closing to your gathering at the last site or back at your church building.*

One: We have seen and felt and prayed with those who are suffering. Holy one, we cry out to you. Hear the prayers of our hearts and our voices.

*Offer additional prayers aloud or in silence.*

One: Let us share the prayer that Jesus has taught us.

*Close with the Lord's Prayer in the language of your community.*

## A HYMN

## BENEDICTION

# INTERLUDE

St. Paul's Episcopal Church was eager to meet with Upper Valley Haven, which provides homeless services in White River Junction, a small town in Vermont. The idea they were meeting about was complicated, but exciting. The church, located near the edge of town, would sell their large parking lot, parsonage, and an adjacent property to the homeless services agency. They would build an overnight shelter and two buildings of permanent low-cost, single-room housing with office space for social workers.

The church would be responsible for building member and neighborhood support, and Upper Valley Haven would guide the project through the zoning process. St. Paul's leadership gathered a team to answer questions from church members and eventually received approval from the congregation to complete the sale. They held informational meetings with the neighborhood, showing off drawings of the planned development and describing the program. The church contacted me to arrange training about how to engage relationally with the new neighbors who would be arriving in the next year.

Along the way things went wrong. The zoning discussion was met with serious questions, and a new plan was needed for the development. Adding to the frustration, the zoning discussion brought attention to the project and suddenly alerted the neighborhood that homeless people would be moving in next door. At the meetings held by the church, small concerns were voiced alongside some support, but attendance was low. However, by this point, the sales contract was already signed, and naysayers living nearby were angry. The discomfort grew, and soon three or four families who were part of the church expressed the feeling that they'd been pressured into agreeing to a bad idea.

The church tried to reassure their neighbors as well as church members, but the plans were in the process of being reworked, and it was unclear exactly what the project would be. This meant clear answers were difficult to provide. Tempers soared, and the church leadership wondered how to move forward. We gathered again to talk about reconciliation and how to create space for those with complaints to say their piece. We also talked about strengthening the biblical foundations for the church's decision to support people who are poor. Eventually, the project went ahead and received the necessary approval.

Now that the buildings are in place, it's hard to remember that it felt like an insurmountable disaster for quite some time. Challenges still exist. People arriving too late for the shelter often sleep in the front doorway of the church since it is protected from the wind. Sometimes people without homes or who are staying at the shelter arrive for church services too early or in rough shape, and they are asked to leave. That wasn't the idea! But overall, the congregation continues to be excited by the opportunity to help. They network with Upper Valley Haven, and most parishioners are willing to receive their occasional visitors with open hearts. The church is even thinking about next steps: creating a cooking program, or a meal program, or a knitting group, or whatever needs they hear about from their new neighbors.

# Epilogue: Easter Morning

I often joke that Easter is the hardest for preaching, because it's the same story every year and everyone is there so you can't say what you did last year. At the same time, there are so many different messages to share on Easter. The Resurrection is good news in many many ways.

For those of us who need more courage, we can see that God stayed with Jesus through the worst of consequences. Things that hurt, even death, are not the end of God's story or our story. One Easter message is that we can have courage because of the Resurrection.

For those of us who see the abundance around us and wish we could help share it more equitably, the Resurrection is a sign that the kingdom of God is at hand. Jesus proclaims this at the start of his ministry, but his death deflates that hope. The miracle of the Resurrection assures us that the good news really is here and being created around us all the time.

For those of us who want to pull our church together to act more faithfully around poverty and wealth, the Easter story is about the way we become the body of Christ. The work continues in this time because each church, each group of people, lives out this work by being the hands, the feet, and the heart of Christ.

Easter, too, includes the promise of forgiveness. In the coming weeks, we'll hear the stories of doubters and the difficulty of recognizing the risen Christ. And then we'll hear the stories of the early church and its stumbles and successes. Whatever we do, when it falls short of Jesus' teaching, his death and Resurrection are signs of God's forgiving spirit.

## Who Will Do This?

The message of our faith is that God will save us. The song "Here I Am Lord" opens with the God of creation hearing people cry out and responding, "My hand will save." We are God's hands in the world. When we hear God's people cry, we must make a choice about whether or not we respond. To hold God's people in our heart requires addressing the poverty in our neighborhoods, our communities, our towns, our states, and our nation. Who shall God send if not us?

# Acknowledgments

Many thanks to Beth Storrs, who kept asking when I was going to write another book, read every chapter twice, and sat with me to talk about poverty and wealth. Many thanks to Steve Godfrey, who read the very early, and very different, first draft and called to say, "This is important." Many thanks to the Bible study at Ashburnham Community Church and Rindge Congregational Church who took part in the first Lenten Study based on this book.